TRANSACTIONS OF THE

AMERICAN PHILOSOPHICAL SOCIETY

HELD AT PHILADELPHIA

FOR PROMOTING USEFUL KNOWLEDGE

VOLUME 73, PART 2, 1983

Lord Lothian and Anglo-American Relations, 1939–1940

DAVID REYNOLDS

Gonville and Caius College, Cambridge University

THE AMERICAN PHILOSOPHICAL SOCIETY

INDEPENDENCE SQUARE: PHILADELPHIA

1983

Library of Congress Catalog
Card Number 82-73836
International Standard Book Number 0–87169–732–7
US ISSN 0065–9746

CONTENTS

		Page
Acknowledgments		v
I.	Lothian's Appointment: For and Against	1
II.	The Phoney War, September 1939–May 1940	9
III.	Lothian and Churchill	15
IV.	The Destroyers Deal	18
V.	Lothian's Failings: The Far Eastern Example	35
VI.	The Origins of Lend-Lease: Lothian's Vindication	39
VII.	Conclusion: Verdict on an Ambassadorship	57
Bibliography		61
Index		64

Lord Lothian at the British Embassy in Washington during his Ambassadorship.

ACKNOWLEDGMENTS

This monograph is related to a larger project on Anglo-American relations in the years before Pearl Harbor which has been published as *The Creation of the Anglo-American Alliance, 1937–1941: A Study in Competitive Co-operation* (London, 1981). My general academic debts are indicated in that book, but I should like to mention here those who have particularly assisted me in preparing the present work.

Although benefiting from the advice and assistance of librarians at all the archives listed in the bibliography, I am especially grateful to Miss M. M. Baird for her help in using the Lothian papers and to Major T. L. Ingram for making available the Hickleton papers. For his interest in the project and for permission to quote from the Lothian papers I should like to thank the present Marquis of Lothian. Other copyright holders who have allowed me to reproduce extracts are the Earl of Halifax (Hickleton papers), the Hon. John Harvey (Harvey diaries), Birmingham University Library (Neville Chamberlain), the British Library of Political and Economic Science (Dalton papers), the Controller of H. M. Stationery Office (Crown Copyright documents), Reading University Library (Nancy Astor papers), the Houghton Library, Harvard University (Moffat diaries), and the Sterling Library, Yale University (Lippmann papers). The Macmillan Press kindly gave permission to reproduce the photograph used in the frontispiece.

Several participants in the events described kindly agreed to be interviewed. I am particularly grateful to Aubrey and Constance Morgan for their time and interest.

My work has been generously supported by grants from H. M. Department of Education and Science, the Master and Fellows of Gonville and Caius College, Cambridge, and the Eleanor Roosevelt Institute. The Center for European Studies, and the Charles Warren Center for Studies in American History, both at Harvard University, have provided convenient and hospitable bases for my research in the USA. I also appreciate the assistance of Patricia McCullaugh and Patricia Denault in typing the manuscript.

For comments on a draft version I wish to thank Professor Warren F. Kimball, Dr. J. A. Thompson, and, not least, my wife Margaret, who has been a constant source of support and encouragement in all my endeavors.

I. Lothian's Appointment: For and Against

Anglo-American relations are too important to be left to the diplomats. That has often been the view taken by British governments during this century, to judge by their choice of ambassadors in Washington. As Max Beloff has written:

The alternation between the professional diplomat and the statesman or man of affairs, which began with the appointment of Bryce [in 1907] and has remained characteristic of Britain's handling of the Washington embassy down to the present day, is perhaps the best indication of the uncertainty that has prevailed as to whether Washington is a foreign capital like any other, or the second centre of an English-speaking world linked to London by ties more significant than those of traditional diplomacy.[1]

Of all the "amateur ambassadors" none was more distinguished than Philip Kerr, eleventh Marquis of Lothian (1882–1940). His tenure of office was brief—August 1939 to December 1940—but it coincided with a crucial period in British and United States history. Historians have long acknowledged Lothian's achievements,[2] and his ambassadorial career was given thoughtful and sympathetic treatment by the official biographer, Sir James Butler.[3] But the recently-opened archives on both sides of the Atlantic enable one to fill in some important gaps and to set Lothian's work in the context of British and United States policy-making. That is one purpose of this monograph. Its wider aim is to show some of the strengths and weaknesses of a non-career diplomat. On the one hand, Lothian's lack of experience and discretion led him into several damaging diplomatic errors. On the other, his understanding of United States politics and his impatience with conventional diplomatic procedures enabled him to bring the two countries closer together at a time when there was considerable hesitancy and mutual suspicion in both capitals. In the end the successes outweighed the failures, as we shall see by examining Lothian's role as intermediary between Churchill and Roosevelt in the two major episodes in Anglo-American diplomacy during 1940, the Destroyers-for-Bases Deal and the origins of Lend-Lease.

Lothian succeeded Sir Ronald Lindsay, who had been British Ambassador in Washington since 1930. Lindsay was the epitome of the old-

---

[1] Max Beloff, *Imperial Sunset: I, Britain's Liberal Empire*, pp. 116–117. Since Professor Beloff wrote this, the controversy over Mr. Peter Jay has given further force to his judgment.

[2] E.g., Winston S. Churchill, *The Second World War*, 2: 354; Cordell Hull, *The Memoirs of Cordell Hull*, 1: 674; H. G. Nicholas, *The United States and Britain* (Chicago, 1975), p. 93.

[3] J. R. M. Butler, *Lord Lothian (Philip Kerr), 1882–1940*, chaps. xiv–xvi. There is also a brief memoir by Sir Edward Grigg in *The American Speeches of Lord Lothian, July 1939 to December 1940* (London, 1941), pp. xvii–xxxix.

school career diplomat—tall, mustachioed, distinguished—cultivating good relations with the president and State Department but keeping out of the public eye. He did little speaking or traveling and did not give a formal press conference until May 1939.[4] Lindsay was acutely shy, but his low profile was a matter of policy as much as preference. He was convinced that efforts to "educate" American opinion were self-defeating. They exacerbated deep American fears that the wily British were trying to entangle the United States in another European war. Only events, as interpreted by the administration and the American media, would have an effect.

The Foreign Office valued Lindsay's services and had on several occasions dissuaded him from retiring. But by May 1938 Lindsay was adamant that a successor had to be found.[5] Initially Lord Halifax, the Foreign Secretary, favored a professional diplomat. One possibility was Sir Robert Vansittart, the former Permanent Under Secretary whose continued presence in the Foreign Office was an embarrassment to both Halifax and Sir Alexander Cadogan, Vansittart's successor as PUS.[6] Another candidate was Sir Miles Lampson, then ambassador in Cairo. But Lampson was already doing an important and delicate job, and, in any case, by July Halifax was not sure that a career man was the best choice. In the words of Oliver Harvey, his private secretary: "He wanted something more striking and original of the Bryce type."[7] Despite keen opposition from both Cadogan and Harvey, Halifax therefore decided to look outside the diplomatic service. First choice was his old friend, Lothian. In early August, Neville Chamberlain, the Prime Minister, and the king gave their approval, and an initially reluctant Lothian formally consented on 12 August.[8]

Although Halifax did not spell out his reasons, these are not difficult to infer. First, Lothian knew America and Americans as well as any living

---

[4] *New York Times*, 19 May, 1939, p. 2. For an account of Lindsay's ambassadorship see Benjamin D. Rhodes, "Sir Ronald Lindsay and the British View from Washington, 1930–1939," in *Essays in Twentieth Century American Diplomatic History dedicated to Professor Daniel M. Smith*, eds. Clifford L. Egan and Alexander W. Knott, pp. 62–89.

[5] Lindsay to Halifax, 23 May 1938, FO 794/17. This file and FO 794/18 are the main sources for this paragraph, supplemented by diary extracts cited below.

[6] *The Diaries of Sir Alexander Cadogan, O.M., 1938–1945*, ed. David Dilks, 20 May 1938, p. 78; *The Diplomatic Diaries of Oliver Harvey, 1937–1940*, ed. John Harvey, 1 June 1938, p. 148.

[7] Harvey, *Diplomatic Diaries*, 11–16 July 1938, p. 163; also 22 April, pp. 128–129. Bryce was the distinguished historian and student of American institutions who had served as ambassador from 1907–1913. For a discussion of his career see Edmund Ions, *James Bryce and American Democracy, 1870–1922*, pp. 199–240.

[8] Cadogan, *Diaries*, 15 June and 29 July 1938, pp. 82–83, 90; Halifax to Chamberlain, 1 August 1938, NC 7/11/32/114; F. R. Hoyer Millar, minute to Cadogan and Harvey, 16 August 1938, FO 794/18.

Chamberlain had left the matter in Halifax's hands. According to Harvey, the premier had said "that as the Americans are so rotten and as it therefore does not matter who we send there he is content to leave the post to the Service." (Harvey, *Diplomatic Diaries*, p. 148, entry for 1 June 1938.) While such a comment squares with Chamberlain's low opinion of the United States, Harvey was reporting it second- or third-hand. Furthermore, he is not a reliable source, especially about people he disliked, such as Chamberlain.

Briton in public life. He had numerous influential friends or close acquaintances, among them Norman Davis, Thomas Lamont, and Felix
Frankfurter. His cousin, Mark Kerr, was an old friend of president Franklin
D. Roosevelt and Lothian had himself talked with the president on several
occasions. Many of these contacts dated from the Paris Peace Conference,
when Lothian had been active as private secretary to Lloyd George, the
British premier. But Lothian also knew other circles of Americans through
his deep commitment to Christian Science and from his work since 1925
as secretary to the Rhodes Trust. In the latter capacity he had traveled
frequently and extensively around the United States; he told reporters in
April 1939 that he had made fourteen visits, covering forty-four states.[9]
Out of these travels grew a remarkable network of acquaintances which
was frequently to amaze his embassy staff. Although strongest among
academics and journalists, it also included business and civic leaders. All
this was in striking contrast with most British policymakers, whose experience of America, where it existed at all, was usually confined to the
East Coast or to the artificial atmosphere of the commercial lecture circuit.

Not only did Lothian know America, he also liked it. While many of
the British elite adopted a condescending attitude to what Harold Nicolson
once called "the eternal superficiality of the American race,"[10] Lothian
found the United States open and invigorating. "I always feel fifteen years
younger when I land in New York," he remarked in 1939.[11] To his un-
feigned, though not uncritical, enthusiasm, many Americans readily responded. They liked his approachable, unpretentious manner, his bespec-
tacled good-looks, his impatience with conventions. Lothian's liberalism—
on such matters as free trade, and constitutional reform in India—was
also appealing, especially when combined with a title, in a country where
the assertion of democratic virtues coexisted with a lingering fascination
with Old World traditions.

Lothian was also well-qualified to take a more forward policy in public
than the one adopted by Lindsay. The embassy's staff, he once observed,
consisted largely "of old public School boys, many of whom manifest a
constitutional inhibition when dealing with the average politician" on
Capitol Hill.[12] He had therefore made it a condition of his appointment
that he be allowed to choose a special attaché to deal with the Washington
press and also to cultivate the contacts with non-official circles in which
the embassy was deficient.[13] Lothian himself was an experienced journalist
and editor. He knew many United States newspapermen, including Walter
Lippmann and William Allen White, and he understood, even enjoyed,

---

[9] *Washington Post*, 26 April 1939, 5: 1.
[10] Nicolson to Vita Sackville-West, 17 November 1934, in Harold Nicolson, *Diaries and Letters*, ed. Nigel Nicolson 1: 189.
[11] Speech in London, 13 July 1939, in Lothian, *American Speeches*, p. xlii.
[12] Lothian (PL) to Lord Stamp, 10 May 1938, LP 367: 884. In England a "Public School" means a private school—the equivalent of an American "prep" school.
[13] PL to Halifax, 8 August 1938 and minute by Hoyer Millar, 16 August 1938, FO 794/18.

the rough-and-tumble of American journalism, which contrasted sharply with the more deferential character of press-government relations in Whitehall. Above all, as we shall see, he appreciated the importance of the media in helping establish that consensus among opinion-leaders upon which any effective American diplomacy has to be based.

Finally, Lothian believed profoundly in the importance of Anglo-American cooperation. Since World War I he had considered this the essential foundation of world peace. His ultimate aim was world government, with regional federations, on the model of a truly federal British Commonwealth, as an intermediate stage.[14] But in the mid-1930s his immediate goals were, to borrow Donald Watt's term, "Atlanticist"—isolation from European commitments and cooperation with the Empire and the United States to promote world peace.[15] Fundamentally, Lothian believed that a strong but peaceful Germany was essential for European stability, and that, if left to themselves, Germany, Italy, and France would maintain a continental equilibrium.[16] This, and his sensitivity to German grievances about the Treaty of Versailles, made him slow to appreciate the extent of Hitler's ambitions, and in 1937–1938 he was identified with the notorious but chimerical "Cliveden Set" of his friend Lady Astor, which left-wing propagandists credited with a baleful, pro-fascist influence over British foreign policy. But by early 1939, convinced that the Führer was "in effect a fanatical gangster," Lothian concluded that a coalition of Western democracies in "resistance to Hitler is the necessary preliminary to a real settlement."[17] Alarm at the Nazi threat strengthened his belief that the United States must assist Britain in policing the world's oceans. This, he argued, Britain had done alone since 1815, in the process underpinning not only her own security but that of the Empire and America. The wooden walls of the Royal Navy had been the ultimate guarantor of the Monroe Doctrine, preventing hostile powers from moving out of European waters into the Atlantic. By the late 1930s, however, the era of the *Pax Britannica* was over. Britain's insular security was threatened by the growth of German air power. Her global position was challenged by a potential coalition of three hostile powers—Germany, Italy, and Japan. America ought therefore to share the burden of controlling the oceans, with the United States in the Pacific and Britain in the Atlantic, so that by deterrence, or if necessary by war, the dictators could be tamed and a new peace system secured.[18]

This was hardly an original or profound theory. Lothian's ideas about

---

[14] These ideas grew out of his experiences with Lord Milner's "Kindergarten," preparing South Africa for Union in 1905–1909, and of the "Round Table" movement that developed from it. For fuller discussion see John E. Kendle, *The Round Table Movement and Imperial Union*.

[15] Donald C. Watt, *Personalities and Policies*, e.g., p. 212.

[16] For a good example, see PL, memo, 4 June 1936, in NC 7/7/4.

[17] Quotations, respectively, from PL to Thomas Lamont, 29 March and to the Aga Khan, 16 May 1939, LP 383: 416 and 388: 14–16.

[18] E.g., PL, article in *The Observer* (London), 19 February 1939, p. 14.

seapower owed much to Alfred T. Mahan and other American naval writers, and were currently being popularized in the United States in the columns of Walter Lippmann. They were also based on a debatable reading of nineteenth-century history. But Lothian was an intellectual rather than a scholar. His gift lay in synthesizing specialist wisdom and using his charm and eloquence to convey it to a wider audience in a neat and plausible form. As one old friend, Thomas Jones, recalled:

Handsome into middle age, untidy, broad-chested, with open gestures, restless arms and hands in and out of his trouser pockets keeping time with his flow of well-turned sentences, positive, assertive, he conveyed a fallacious lucidity of one who had done the thinking and solved the difficulties for you.[19]

Moreover, he argued the case for Anglo-American cooperation not from sentiment or from Britain's needs, as many of his countrymen were wont to do, but from the standpoint of America's own security. This ability to appreciate the American point of view was one of his distinctive characteristics. As he explained to a farewell dinner in London in July 1939, he conceived it to be his task "not merely to represent the policy of the British Government to the Administration in Washington and vice versa, but to increase the mutual comprehension between the two peoples. . . ."[20] We shall see that this concept of "mutual education" was to be the basic theme of his ambassadorship.

Halifax had hoped that Lothian could take up his post in the autumn of 1938, but Lothian's commitments in Australia and then the king's desire to retain the experienced Lindsay to oversee the royal visit to the United States the following June necessitated a long delay. The appointment was therefore unannounced, and unknown to all but a handful of senior British policymakers, throughout the winter. The State Department was naturally aware that Lindsay was due to retire, but the first direct intimation came on 26 October 1938 when Lindsay told Sumner Welles, the undersecretary of state, that his departure was imminent.[21] It was presumably because of this that Norman Davis wrote to Cadogan on November 14 to say that

While Lindsay has been a real success here in every respect, it is felt in certain quarters that unless it is possible to get an exceptional Service man, it would be highly beneficial to have someone with practical political experience who is or has been a Cabinet Officer and is thus well known, and who could, on occasion, make a good speech.[22]

Davis stressed that this was a personal letter, but, in view of his close relationship with Roosevelt and of his previous role as an Anglo-American

---

[19] Thomas Jones to Violet Markham, 18 February 1944, in Thomas Jones, *A Diary with Letters, 1931–1950.* p. 515.

[20] PL, *American Speeches*, p. xli.

[21] Memo of conversation between Welles and Lindsay, 26 October 1938, D/S 841.001 George VI/267½. (This was before Lindsay was asked to stay on for the royal visit.)

[22] Davis to Cadogan, 14 November 1938, Norman H. Davis papers, box 8, folder "C" (LC).

go-between, it is likely that this was a gentle hint from the White House. More direct advice came via Lord Tweedsmuir, the Governor General of Canada, who told Chamberlain in January that Roosevelt considered the choice of Lindsay's successor "enormously important," adding that the president thought "that a career-diplomat is not the proper choice at this time."[23] The British took note of these judgments, which of course coincided with their own, but there is no evidence that they revealed the identity of Lindsay's successor to the administration before the end of March.

When Lothian visited the United States for seven weeks from Christmas 1938, his status was therefore still that of a private citizen. He came to make secret arrangements to replace Lindsay and to assess America's mood after Munich. Alarmed at German aggression and United States unpreparedness, he also intended to put the need for rearmament and for Anglo-American cooperation starkly before American leaders, including the president.[24] In correspondence and at various private gatherings in Washington he therefore insisted that Britain could not maintain the world balance alone, that America must take up the role of policing the oceans, and that the struggle between dictatorship and democracy was effectively a duel between Hitler and Roosevelt.[25] It was in the same vein that he spoke with Roosevelt on 2 January.

The two men found a substantial area of agreement. Lothian now accepted that Hitler must be tamed before peace could be secured, and he had to endure considerable teasing from Roosevelt about his earlier credulity. The president, for his part, was anxious to accelerate American air rearmament, to act as democracy's arsenal and to use United States diplomatic influence as pressure upon the dictators. Where they differed was in their perception of the Anglo-American relationship. Lothian believed that the United States must assume Britain's role as guardian of world peace, arguing that Britain no longer had the power to do this herself. Not all British leaders were as keen on Anglo-American cooperation as Lothian, but they agreed that at least temporarily Britain's resources did not match her global responsibilities. Roosevelt, by contrast, saw Britain's problem as a lack of nerve rather than a lack of power. He complained to his

---

[23] Tweedsmuir to Chamberlain, 23 January 1939, NC 7/11/32/280. On 18 November 1938, FDR discussed the question with Mackenzie King, the Canadian premier. At this stage he had heard rumors that Whitehall intended to send a career diplomat, Sir Hughe Knatchbull-Hugessen. According to King, Roosevelt "said how can a man with a name like that ever get his personality across this country. . . . He then said he wished the British would send someone like Walter Elliott or Malcolm MacDonald [respectively Conservative and National Labour MPs who were both ministers in Chamberlain's National Government]." King passed on FDR's remarks to Tweedsmuir, though he felt that the Governor General did not take the point. W. L. Mackenzie King, Diary, entries for 17 November 1938, p. 11, and 20 November 1938, p. 3 (Public Archives of Canada, Ottawa).

[24] Cf. PL to Lloyd George, 16 December 1938, David Lloyd George papers, G/12/5/67 (HLRO).

[25] E.g., PL to FDR, 1 February 1939, PPF 5731; Jay Pierrepont Moffat, diary, 5 January and 4 February (Houghton Library, Harvard University); PL memo of 7 February 1939, in Davis papers, box 40.

associates that Lothian's remarks were typical of the spineless, buck-passing attitude currently taken by the British.[26] His reactions clearly reveal the limited conception of America's world role which he entertained at this stage. America would help redress the current military imbalance, but she would not be pushed into a position of international leadership or dragged into another war. The primary responsibility for world peace lay on Britain's shoulders, and, once the backbones of her timorous leaders had been suitably stiffened, he believed those shoulders would be equal to the task.

On various occasions during the winter, the president tried to make his policy clear to the British government,[27] and Lothian's remarks provided a convenient illustration. When Roosevelt's old Harvard professor, Roger B. Merriman, sent him part of a dispirited letter from the British historian G. M. Trevelyan, Roosevelt's reply was brief but impassioned. He told Merriman on 15 February 1939:

I wish the British would stop this "We who are about to die, salute thee" attitude. Lord Lothian was here the other day, started the conversation by saying he had completely abandoned his former belief that Hitler could be dealt with as a semireasonable human being, and went on to say that the British for a thousand years had been the guardians of Anglo-Saxon civilization—that the scepter or the sword or something like that had dropped from their palsied fingers—that the U.S.A. must snatch it up—that F.D.R. alone could save the world—etc., etc.

I got mad clear through and told him that just so long as he or Britishers like him took that attitude of complete despair, the British would not be worth saving anyway.

What the British need today is a good stiff grog, inducing not only the desire to save civilization but the continued belief that they can do it. In such an event they will have a lot more support from their American cousins—don't you think so?[28]

Merriman inferred that he was to pass on Roosevelt's observations to the British. He sent a copy to Trevelyan for his discreet use, which Trevelyan in turn forwarded to Halifax at the Foreign Office. Roosevelt's point, of course, was to stiffen British policy. There is no evidence that he knew of Lothian's selection or that he wanted to alter it. Indeed Lothian fitted well the criteria suggested by him via Davis and Tweedsmuir. But senior

---

[26] Notes by Josephus Daniels, 14 January 1939, copy in PPF 86/2; *The Secret Diary of Harold L. Ickes* 3 vols., (1954), 2: 571, on conversation on 28 January 1939; *The Forrestal Diaries*, ed. Walter Millis, p. 122, entry for 27 December 1945.

[27] For fuller details on FDR's policy see David Reynolds, *The Creation of the Anglo-American Alliance, 1937–1941: A Study in Competitive Co-operation* (1981), pp. 40–44.

[28] FDR to Merriman, 15 February 1939, PSF 46: GB, 1939. Lothian later claimed that the meeting was "extremely friendly." Roosevelt, he said, "in no way indicated the point of view he mentions in his letter to Merriman. I was particularly careful to avoid anything which looked like saying what I thought the United States ought to do because that clearly was not my business. . . ." (PL to Lindsay, 31 March 1939, LP 383: 445–447.) Of course, Lothian was anxious to play down the episode, but it is likely, knowing Roosevelt, that he maintained his affability during the interview, blew off steam to his associates later, and exaggerated his account of the meeting to make his basic point more effectively.

officials in the Foreign Office, led by Cadogan, seized on the letter as an opportunity to overturn an appointment they had consistently disliked. In the light of Roosevelt's comments both Chamberlain and the king were also doubtful about the wisdom of sending Lothian, but Halifax, backed by Lindsay, stuck to his guns. In the end Lindsay was instructed to ask Roosevelt directly for his opinion of Lothian. On 28 March the president made it clear that he had nothing against him, stating bluntly: "Look here, there can be no possible difficulty about his *agrément* or anything of that sort."[29] Public announcement of the appointment was made on 24 April, and, after further delays, Lothian finally took up his post at the end of August 1939.

It is worth dwelling for a moment on the controversy in Whitehall over Roosevelt's letter. The senior Foreign Office officials opposed Lothian in large measure because they wished to keep the job within the diplomatic service. Resentful of any outsider carrying off the "plum" posts, they particularly disliked Lothian for his repeated interference in foreign affairs right back to his days as Lloyd George's *éminence grise*. But reinforcing bureaucratic self-interest were genuine doubts about Lothian's suitability. For one thing, they feared that his well-publicized sympathy for Germany might prove an embarrassment in the United States, where the "Cliveden Set" had become a prevalent myth.[30] More fundamental still, there were reservations about his discretion and judgment. A highly-strung, somewhat neurotic bachelor, Lothian tended to be carried away by his current mood and immediate situation. Even his friends admitted that this was a weakness, and senior Foreign Office officials were outspoken in their criticism. An "incurably superficial Johnny-know-all" was Vansittart's scathing comment in 1935 after Lothian's first visit to Hitler.[31] The Roosevelt-Merriman letter seemed confirmation of these defects. As Cadogan pointed out, it made a mockery of Lothian's brash confidence that on his recent visit he had "put it across" America and was "swinging" opinion there. It also showed his apparent insensitivity to the delicacy of the problem, in striking contrast with Lindsay's discretion.[32] Although these doubts were eventually overruled, they are nevertheless significant. The episode of the Roosevelt letter revealed the other side of Lothian—those facets of his character and experience that were to prove a weakness in a vital but delicate diplomatic mission.

---

[29] Lindsay to Halifax, 29 March 1938, FO 794/18. For fuller discussion of the material in his paragraph see David Reynolds, "FDR on the British: A postscript," 106–110.

[30] Cf. Cadogan, *Diaries*, 15 December 1938, p. 130; Scott, minute, 7 March 1939, FO 794/18.

[31] Minute of 2 February 1935, quoted in W. N. Medlicott, *Britain and Germany: The Search for Agreement, 1930–1937*, p. 12, note 3.

[32] Cadogan to Halifax, 1 March 1939, FO 794/18 and Cadogan, *Diaries*, 2 March, p. 154.

II. The Phoney War, September, 1939–May, 1940

The first phase of Lothian's ambassadorship may conveniently be said to span the period of the Phoney War (September 1939–May 1940). During these months his influence in both countries was limited. Four main reasons may be discerned for this.

First, Lothian's enthusiasm for Anglo-American cooperation was not shared at the top of British government. While not indifferent to the United States, and well aware that in the event of total war Britain would need large-scale American help, Chamberlain and his immediate advisers had little hope that the United States could be relied upon. From bitter experience they had learned that the promises of American presidents could easily be repudiated by Congress or public. Furthermore, efforts to "educate" America out of her entrenched isolation seemed self-defeating. The sure way to lose the Americans, Chamberlain told Labour critics in June 1939, was to run after them too hard.[33] But there was more to Whitehall's policy than this ingrained doubt. The British, after all, were fighting not only for their security against Hitler but also for their continued position as a world power. To triumph over Hitler by becoming dependent upon the United States would be a pyrrhic victory, tantamount to defeat. At the back of their minds was the memory of the Great War, when America had profited from her neutrality to capture Britain's trade and had tried to enforce her conception of world order on victors as well as vanquished. For Chamberlain the lessons were clear. He wanted benevolent United States neutrality (diplomatic assistance and limited material support) *if* that could be achieved. He did not want American entry into the war. "Heaven knows," he wrote in January 1940, "I don't want the Americans to fight for us—we should have to pay too dearly for that if they had a right to be in on the peace terms. . . ."[34]

Second, there was the character of the "Phoney War." Today it seems like the unreal calm before the inevitable storm—the muted prelude to eventual world war. But one must remember that after the Polish collapse in 1939, the conflict was, and seemed likely to remain, confined to Western Europe. The U.S.A., U.S.S.R., Japan, and Italy remained in varying degrees of neutrality. In fact the main British anxiety that winter was to keep the war out of the Mediterranean. The crucial neutrals were Italy and the Balkan States, rather than the United States. Furthermore, no one knew

---

[33] Hugh Dalton, diary, 28 June 1939 (British Library of Political and Economic Science, London).

[34] NC to Ida Chamberlain, 27 January 1940, NC 18/1/1140. See also Reynolds, *Creation of the Anglo-American Alliance*, pp. 73–83.

9

how long the conflict might last. Officially the Allies were preparing for a protracted war of attrition, judging that if they could resist the initial German offensive, then in the long run, through bombing, blockade, and application of their superior global economic resources, they could force the Germans to overthrow Hitler and negotiate an acceptable peace. It was therefore essential to conserve Britain's gold and foreign exchange reserves for a long struggle. But privately Chamberlain and many leading policymakers hoped that the war might be over quickly. Convinced that the German economy was already overstretched and unaware of Hitler's Blitzkrieg strategy of short, sharp campaigns supplied by an only partially mobilized economy, they remained alert for signs of an early German collapse. This belief that the war might be a short one strengthened Chamberlain's hope that he could avoid major changes in the status quo, including reliance upon America.

Lothian was further constrained by the need to establish his credibility as ambassador in the eyes of the Foreign Office. He had to improve his not-unjustified image as a cocky intellectual, contemptuous of hide-bound professional diplomats. This proved a slow process. One senior Foreign Office minister remarked in mid-September that "Lothian seemed to be getting on pretty well with the President, and his despatches were not, as might have been expected, too verbose."[35] But not everyone agreed. After trying to elucidate the meaning of one "rather contradictory" and "rather impalpable" letter in November, Cadogan dismissed Lothian as "a phrase-monger," and in December the United States Ambassador in London, Joseph Kennedy, told the State Department that the Foreign Office was "still hesitant in its judgment" of the new ambassador.[36] Now the Foreign Office, and particularly its American Department, was potentially Lothian's best ally in Whitehall. Although most British policymakers entertained the ingrained doubts and nagging fears about America, such feelings were particularly associated with Chamberlain, his Treasury advisers and Tory backbenchers, together with certain senior Foreign Office officials such as Cadogan. Halifax and, naturally, Foreign Office/American Department were keener to promote Anglo-American cooperation. The initial Foreign Office coolness towards Lothian was therefore an obstacle to his effective influence on British policy.

Finally, Lothian had to take account of the very delicate state of American opinion. Lindsay had tried to make him aware of this during the summer. He urged Lothian to avoid public statements and shelve all plans for improved publicity in the U.S.A. until he had had a chance to judge the situation for himself. Reluctantly Lothian accepted this advice, declining speaking engagements and postponing arrangements, which he had already begun, to find a suitable press attaché.[37] On arriving in the

---

[35] R. A. Butler, in Dalton diary, 18 September 1939.

[36] Cadogan, minute, no date, FO 800/317, p. 229, and *Diaries*, 27 November 1939, p. 234; Moffat diary, 8 December 1939.

[37] Lindsay to PL, 16 May 1939, LP 392: 402–404; also correspondence in LP 392: 425–426, 390: 259–263 and FO 395/657, P3115, P3240/151/150.

United States, he appreciated the reason for Lindsay's caution. During the autumn 1939 Roosevelt was engaged in securing repeal of the arms embargo. This prohibited the sale of arms, ammunition and munitions to the belligerents. Instead he wanted a blanket "cash and carry" law, by which belligerents could purchase without restriction in the United States, provided that they paid immediately for the goods and carried them away in their own ships. The intent of the cash and carry policy was to avoid the economic entanglements and naval incidents that, supposedly, had led to United States involvement in the Great War, while at the same time allowing the Allies, with their superior navies and greater foreign exchange, preferential access to the American market. It was not simply a compromise with the strength of congressional isolation, but also an expression of the limited liability policy expounded by the president the previous winter. This was therefore an inopportune moment for a British ambassador to start "educating" Americans about Anglo-American cooperation against Hitler. As Lothian told the Foreign Office less than a fortnight after his arrival in Washington: "We have clearly got to go very slowly in this country for the next few weeks."[38] In fact, caution was the watchword for much of the winter. Lothian therefore confined himself to building up relations with the president and State Department, and kept a low profile on Capitol Hill. Although preparing contingency plans for improving British publicity, he insisted that nothing should be done until American opinion became less sensitive about "propaganda."

But Lothian had not completely abandoned his plans for promoting Anglo-American cooperation. His speechmaking provides the clearest evidence of this. During the Phoney War he gave eleven addresses, all of them referring in some way to the international scene.[39] To counter head-on the possible accusation of propagandizing, Lothian usually reminded his audience of the American commitment to freedom of speech and information, explaining that he was only presenting the facts, and a British interpretation of them, from which Americans could make up their own minds. In these speeches he expounded his philosophy of international affairs, in a form calculated to appeal to American interests and ideals. He emphasized that Britain was fighting for the fundamental values of liberalism and democracy, that she was the center not of an old-fashioned empire but an evolving, self-governing commonwealth. He reiterated the importance of the Anglo-American division of seapower, noting how United States security in the Atlantic was bound up with the survival of the British fleet. He also speculated about the new post-war order for which the Allies were fighting and suggested the need for European and world federation on a commonwealth model.

In all this Lothian's real aim was not to convert his immediate listeners (he was an indifferent formal public speaker) but to get his ideas disseminated by the media to a much wider audience. Lothian had made himself

---

[38] PL to FO, tel. 443, 8 September 1939, FO 371/22816, A6155/98/45.
[39] See lists in LP 408: 1. For texts of major speeches see PL, *American Speeches*, pp. 1–87.

readily accessible to ordinary journalists, both individually and through informal press conferences in the Roosevelt manner. Copies of his speeches were printed and widely distributed—usually about 2,500 in the case of the major addresses.[40] Lothian himself made sure they reached public figures, especially the leading sympathetic newspaper-owners, such as Arthur Hays Sulzberger of the *New York Times*, the Ogden Reids of the *New York Herald Tribune*, and Eugene Meyer of the *Washington Post*, with whom he was soon on good terms. All but traditionally anti-British papers responded very favorably to his speeches. They quoted from them extensively and went on, as Lothian had hoped, to debate the ideas he had thrown out in editorials and syndicated columns for days afterwards. His idealism appealed to an American media disenchanted with the apparent cynicism of British diplomacy in the 1930s and suspicious of the "phoney" war. A speech in Chicago in January 1940 attracted particular attention and praise. The columnist Dorothy Thompson, for instance, called it "the clearest statement of British war and peace aims which has yet been made anywhere."[41]

However, comments like this caused alarm in London. Even sympathetic friends advised Lothian to "go slow" on such questions as world federation.[42] In the Foreign Office/American Department one official, Victor Perowne, took it upon himself to scrutinize Lothian's speeches with a zeal far beyond the call of duty which must have reflected both personal and ideological animus. He drew attention to the fact that the ambassador's speeches were being taken in the United States as official British policy, while, in the House of Commons, the references to federalism, and Anglo-American control of the seas had upset some senior backbenchers with long memories of Wilson and of the naval rivalry of the 1920s. Although Perowne's superiors did not fully share his anxiety about the content of Lothian's speeches, they did feel that he should still be very discreet in public. Some also questioned his conception of the ambassador's role. David Scott, the assistant undersecretary with oversight of Foreign Office/American Department, felt that the ambassador's task was principally to "jolly along" the State Department "by emitting a pleasant odour" and not to resort to overt pressure or public lecturing. Although not particularly worried, Halifax was persuaded to administer a gentle rebuke.[43] Lothian's reply is interesting. In it he made clear that he was trying to educate not one but two audiences—3,000 miles apart. The postwar world would require changes in British as well as American attitudes, he suggested. Americans would only participate in a world organization when they saw that Europe was trying to regulate its own affairs through

---

[40] Cf. LP 405: 8.

[41] *New York Herald Tribune*, 8 January 1940, p. 13.

[42] E.g., R. H. Brand to PL, 5 December 1939, LP 399: 183–184.

[43] See FO 371/24246, A772/301/45, esp. minutes by Perowne and Scott, 20 and 23 January, and Halifax to PL, 30 January 1940. According to Halifax, Churchill had recently said that "to ask a Cabinet minister to make a speech without causing offence in some quarter is like telling a centipede to go for a walk and not to put his foot in it!"

some kind of continental federation. Similarly, an effective system of collective naval security required not only United States involvement but a readiness on the part of the British, including Halifax's "die-hard friends" in Parliament, to share naval power with the United States.[44]

By late January 1940 Lothian's abilities as a "mutual educator" were sorely needed. There was growing tension between the two countries. In part the problem was simply another of the recurrent Anglo-American clashes about belligerent versus neutral rights, which arose every time there was a European war. The British considered the blockade their decisive weapon and they enforced it with increasing determination. This led to disputes with the U.S.A. about such matters as mail censorship and inspection of United States merchant shipping for contraband. However, it was not simply the blockade that caused the offense, but the inequities in its operation. Anxious to keep the Mediterranean quiet, Britain had accorded preferential treatment to Italian shipping and had agreed to buy Italian and Balkan agricultural produce at a time when it was reducing such purchases from the United States. This greatly angered fruit, cotton, and tobacco producers in the South, whose support was essential to the Democratic coalition and to Roosevelt's effective leadership in Congress. Some officials in the State Department saw a deeper and more sinister motive behind British policy. They judged that it was part of a general attempt to create a closed British trading bloc, based on the Sterling Area and the Empire. In consequence they made repeated protests about Whitehall's actions and, when no satisfactory response was forthcoming, they leaked their dissatisfaction to the media in an effort to apply pressure.

Lothian did his best to conciliate the State Department, but fundamentally he accepted that United States grievances were justified. He explained to London that they were part of a general shift of American opinion about the war. The United States, he said, was still anxious to see Hitler defeated, while keeping out of the war herself. But now that the inactivity on the Western Front had dispelled earlier fears that America would quickly be drawn in, Americans were determined to assert their rights and interests more vigorously. In part, he advised, the remedy lay in proper explanation of British policy. Britain could not assume acquiescence, but if the Administration and public could be convinced "that any action we take affecting them is really necessary for the winning of the war" then they would cooperate.[45] This was a constant theme for the next few months. But Lothian also called for a change in the content as well as the form of British policy. He advised Britain to resume agricultural purchases in the U.S.A., if only on a token basis to prove her goodwill. It should

---

[44] PL to Halifax, 11 March 1940, FO 800/324, pp. 238–241. In the letter Lothian commented: "I can imagine what my speeches would have been like if they had first been minuted by all veterans of the Foreign Office at home!" The letter was marked "private and personal" but a copy found its way into FO/A files (see FO 371/24246, A2314/301/45) and Lothian's comment can have done nothing to endear him to its officials.

[45] PL to Halifax, 27 January 1940, FO 800/324, H/XXXVII/44, circulated to the Cabinet as WP(G) (40) 30 in CAB 67/4.

also give firm assurances that the wartime restrictions were only temporary and did not indicate an embryonic autarkic trading bloc. Lothian's pleas had some success. Backed by Foreign Office/American Department, he obliged Chamberlain to restate publicly Britain's commitment to post-war multilateral trade.[46] But the Cabinet remained reluctant to spend scarce dollars in the U.S.A. There was general agreement that Britain must conserve her foreign exchange, and that if exceptions had to be made, the Mediterranean neutrals were of prime importance. Even Halifax, anxious about American opinion, took this view.[47] Behind it lay not only the policy of financial caution for a long war, but the persistent hope, entertained particularly by Chamberlain and his immediate advisers, that the war could be won without major diminution of Britain's wealth and power. Until such attitudes changed, Lothian's influence on British policy was inevitably peripheral.

---

[46] See esp. FO 371/25052, W1508/2/49 and FO 371/25069, W1538/8/49.
[47] CAB 65/5, WM 26 (40) 1, 29 January 1940.

III. Lothian and Churchill

From May 1940 on Lothian played a major role in Anglo-American relations. In part this new importance reflected the work he had put in during the winter in gradually gaining the trust of the Foreign Office and the Roosevelt Administration.[48] His dispatches about United States opinion were considered models of analysis,[49] and, although Perowne maintained an aggressive vigilance, most Foreign Office officials were increasingly impressed with his speeches.[50] But it was the dramatic changes of May–June 1940 that really brought Lothian to prominence. Both British and American policy had rested on the assumption that the French army was their secure first line of defense. The rapid collapse of the Western Front left both countries nearly defenseless. Britain was dependent on United States help, while American leaders feared that only the British fleet lay between them and Hitler's rampaging armies. The two countries were therefore forced into closer commitments.

Changes in the British leadership reinforced this change in events. As Europe fell into German hands and America emerged as the crucial neutral, so the American Department assumed a new importance within the Foreign Office's policymaking process. Working well now with Lothian, it relayed and amplified his views to British leaders. Even more important, Churchill replaced Chamberlain as premier. Although not immune from the doubts and suspicions of America that infected all the British elite to some extent, the new Prime Minister was far more enthusiastic than his predecessor about an Anglo-American alliance. He was also much readier than Chamberlain to interfere in the detailed handling of foreign policy, particularly where the United States was concerned. Gradually an effective working relationship was created between Churchill, Foreign Office/ American Department and Lothian, which brought Anglo-American issues to the center of British policymaking.

---

[48] Lindsay learned in May from Bill Bullitt, Roosevelt's friend and ambassador in Paris, "that Lothian is doing magnificently in Washington. The President likes him and was always pleased to see him, which was rare as he found most people bores...." (Lindsay to Cadogan, 25 May 1940, FO 794/18.)

[49] For example, a dispatch from PL on 1 February 1940, was considered "an excellent survey" by FO/A. The king's private secretary, who saw a great many such missives, described it as "the best I have ever seen from an ambassadorial pen." (See minutes on copy in FO 371/24238, A1190/131/45; Sir Alan Lascelles to PL, 12 March 1940, FO 800/398, Mis/40/3.)

[50] In May, a senior FO official who had recently spent several weeks in Washington reported that while in general Britons should avoid speechmaking in the United States, "in the case of Lord Lothian's speeches, both big and small, I have heard nothing but praise. It is not every British speaker who knows how to address American audiences." (Frank Ashton-Gwatkin to FO, 19 May 1940, FO 371/25143, W8233/79/49).

This process was not without its difficulties, however, and it is worth looking for a moment at Lothian's relationship with Churchill—the mercurial political maverick who had spent the previous decade in the wilderness. When war began, Lothian welcomed Churchill's return to power as First Lord of the Admiralty. For some time he had been keen to see Churchill brought into the Cabinet, not least for the effect this would have on opinion in the United States.[51] Nevertheless, like most of Whitehall, his feelings were ambivalent. According to a State Department official in September, Lothian felt "that nine days out of ten Churchill was magnificent, but the tenth day during a crisis he was apt to lose his head, close his ears, and refuse to listen to reason . . . Despite this weakness, Lothian felt that he had the exuberance, drive and leadership which England craved."[52] Lothian also believed that Churchill's periodic follies had prevented him from attaining the premiership. In the political crisis of early May 1940 he saw no obvious successor to Chamberlain and even when Churchill took office Lothian feared, like many in Whitehall, that he would accept no advice and would become "a dictator."[53] Until his private papers are fully open, it is less easy to ascertain Churchill's attitude to Lothian. But the comments in Sir Winston's war memoirs are probably a reliable guide. There Churchill noted that "we had differed much and often from Versailles to Munich and later," and that Lothian "had given me the impression of high intellectual and aristocratic detachment from vulgar affairs."[54] Presumably their differences in the 1930s over India and above all Germany were much in his mind.

There was consequently considerable mutual hesitancy to overcome. Moreover, the two men had clashed on several occasions during 1939 and 1940 over Churchill's secret correspondence with Roosevelt. This had begun in October 1939, when Churchill, with Chamberlain's approval, followed up the president's invitation to them both to keep him informed personally and informally about any problems or matters of interest. During the Phoney War the messages were few in number and confined to naval affairs, but after Churchill's assumption of the premiership they gradually developed into a wide-ranging and crucial line of communication. Churchill was determined that this should be a personal and private correspondence. He preferred to send messages through Ambassador Kennedy and the State Department, rather than via the Foreign Office and Lothian, which, he apparently felt, would make them seem like ordinary diplomatic traffic. Neither Foreign Office/American Department nor Lothian knew of some of the earliest messages, and the ambassador was embarrassed to find the State Department treating telegrams of which he was

[51] Cf. PL to J. L. Garvin, 5 July 1939, LP 390: 258 and Johnson to Hull, disp. 3072, p. 3, 22 July 1939, D/S 841.00/1423.

[52] Moffat diary, 26 September 1939.

[53] See PL to Herbert Bayard Swope, 22 March 1940 and to Frances Stevenson, 14 May 1940 ("dictator"), LP 405: 269, 161; also Moffat diary, 2 May 1940.

[54] Churchill, *Second World War*, 2: 354, 490.

unaware as authoritative statements of British policy.[55] After representations from Halifax and Foreign Office/American Department Churchill agreed in January 1940 that copies of subsequent messages would be sent for information to the Washington Embassy, "thus keeping Lothian fully informed while giving the President the feeling that he has a special line of information."[56] This arrangement lasted until late May when, following a major security leak in the United States Embassy, Churchill agreed to communicate solely via Lothian. But after two weeks he reverted to the former procedure. Lothian protested anew, pointing out that the president was so busy that unless there was a message from Churchill to deliver it was difficult for him to gain access. Eventually it was agreed in July that some cables should be sent via Lothian and some via Kennedy, the method of transmission to be determined by Churchill in each case. This practice was preserved for the remainder of Lothian's ambassadorship.[57] The significance of the controversy was that the correspondence threatened to undermine Lothian's position as trusted intermediary between London and Washington, in the way that Roosevelt's use of special emissaries such as Norman Davis and Harry Hopkins weakened the authority of his own ambassadors in London. Information is influence, and Lothian fought tenaciously and successfully to maintain his status as the major channel between the two leaders.[58]

---

[55] PL to FO, tels. 635, 775, 19 October and 17 November 1939, FO 371/22764, A8146/5992/51.

[56] Halifax to WSC, 19 January 1940, ADM 199/1928.

[57] See papers in FO 371/24192, A3261/1/51, and in PREM 4/27/3. For a summary of the whole controversy see Llewellyn Woodward, *British Foreign Policy in the Second World War* 1: 334–335 note, and, more generally, James Leutze, "The Secret of the Churchill-Roosevelt Correspondence: September 1939–May 1940," pp. 465–491.

[58] He was also protected by Halifax. On 20 June 1940, prompted by criticisms of Lothian and his appeasing past, Churchill suggested that "there is something to be said for a strong mission to the United States" to handle all threads of Anglo-American relations—diplomatic, military, financial, supply, etc. (Perhaps he had in mind the Balfour mission of 1917?) Halifax responded firmly: "Personally, I have confidence in Lothian. I doubt the necessity of a 'strong mission' alongside of him, and fear that it might be embarrassing, if not perhaps a little unfair to him, and might produce some confusion." (WSC to Halifax, and Halifax to WSC, 20 and 21 June 1940, PREM 4/25/8, pp. 700, 699.)

IV. The Destroyers Deal

Lothian's effectiveness in this role can best be judged by examining his part in the celebrated Destroyers Deal, concluded on 2 September 1940 after months of negotiation. The British were to receive fifty World War I United States destroyers in return for ninety-nine year leases of land on eight British possessions in the Western Atlantic and the Caribbean on which the United States could construct naval and air bases. Whitehall also publicly stated that, in the event that Britain fell, the Royal Navy would not be sunk or surrendered. The diplomacy leading up to these agreements fell into three main stages: the period from mid-May to mid-June when the French surrendered, during which Britain's need for United States destroyers and the Administration's anxiety about the future of the British fleet were the main subjects of argument; the next six weeks when Roosevelt was immersed in domestic politics prior to his renomination and both he and Churchill waited to see whether Britain could survive alone; and the final month of August when a complicated deal involving destroyers, bases, and an assurance about the Royal Navy was evolved.[59]

On 15 May, in his first message on becoming premier, Churchill put United States destroyers at the top of his "shopping list" to Roosevelt. The following day the president explained that America needed all her destroyers for patrolling her coasts and that, in any case, they could not be sold without congressional approval, which would not be forthcoming. On 17 May Lothian applied the pressure in a significant conversation with the president. He outlined the naval crisis that would face the U.S.A. if Britain collapsed for want of American help. With the main United States fleet at Hawaii to deter Japan, and only a weak Atlantic squadron on the East Coast, the United States would have to face naval threats in both oceans. Responding, Roosevelt suggested that if the worst happened, the British fleet might cross the Atlantic to Canada or the U.S.A. Lothian replied that this would probably depend on whether the United States had entered the war. He did not think British public opinion would entrust the fleet to a neutral America. The president, Lothian told London, "seemed impressed by this possibility."[60]

---

[59] The standard study is Philip Goodhart, *Fifty Ships that Saved the World: The Foundation of the Anglo-American Alliance*. See also the more recent accounts in Woodward, *British Foreign Policy*, 1: chaps XI–XII; the important book by James R. Leutze, *Bargaining for Supremacy: Anglo-American Naval Collaboration, 1937–1941*, chaps. 6–8; Reynolds, *Creation of the Anglo-American Alliance*, chaps. 4–5.

[60] PL to FO, tel. 759, 18 May 1940, A3261. This file also contains copies of the FDR-WSC cables.

As James Leutze has convincingly shown, this conversation set the guidelines for British and American tactics over the next few weeks. While Roosevelt emphasized the importance of preserving the French and British fleets whatever happened in Europe, Lothian reiterated his warning that Britain was unlikely to entrust its navy to a neutral America. Churchill, too, took up the theme, often adding a sinister twist of his own: his own ministry would fight to the end, but if Britain fell and the United States was not an ally then a peacemaking government might surrender the fleet to secure better terms. Professor Leutze suggests that Britain's tactics were "maladroit" and counter-productive—focusing Roosevelt's attention on the possibility of a British collapse and showing an insensitivity to his own domestic difficulties which made a declaration of war impossible.[61]

There is much truth in these judgments. The British were in a panicky mood in May and June, casting desperately around for any way of pressing the Americans. But we need to remember Britain's ingrained doubt about the United States—the conviction that only with difficulty could Americans be moved to effective action. In May 1940, Whitehall felt strongly that Britain was fighting America's battle and that the United States was doing virtually nothing to help. Roosevelt's harping on the future of the fleet only increased British resentment, and encouraged them to repeat their own warnings. On 27 May, for instance, while the British army was trapped around Dunkirk, the Cabinet felt that Roosevelt "seemed to be taking the view that it would be nice of him to pick up the pieces of the British Empire if this country was overrun. It was as well that he should realize that there was another aspect of the question."[62] Three days later Lothian reported that over the previous week Roosevelt's anxiety about the British fleet had apparently lessened, because, Lothian judged, he had persuaded himself that the British Dominions could be relied upon to get the fleet across the Atlantic before it was too late. This, Lothian believed, was the president's "paralysing illusion"; his confidence about getting the fleet made him feel it was unnecessary to provide aid to Britain. Shrewdly Lothian emphasized that Roosevelt was hedging his bets: "The expert politician in the President is always trying to find a way of winning the war for the Allies, or, if he fails to do that, of ensuring the security of the United States, without the United States itself having to take the plunge into the war."[63]

In view of British scepticism and of reports like this from Lothian, it is hardly surprising that Churchill continued to play on Roosevelt's fears about the fleet. The object was to make clear that the vital battle was taking place in Europe. If Americans did not provide adequate support

---

[61] Leutze, *Bargaining for Supremacy*, chap. 6, esp. p. 91.

[62] CAB 65/13, p. 181, WM 142 (40) CA, 27 May 1940.

[63] PL to FO, tel 868, 30 May 1940, A3261. According to Leutze, *Bargaining for Supremacy*, p. 75, Lothian believed that what paralyzed Roosevelt was his fear that the fleet would be lost. This seems an incorrect reading of the telegram—cf. Woodward, *British Foreign Policy* 1: 343.

for Britain and France, they would not have a second chance to defend themselves in the Western Hemisphere, reinforced by the British fleet. It is also important to note that Churchill restricted his gloomy warnings about the fleet to private messages for American leaders. In public he maintained a mood of indefatigable optimism to uplift morale at home and abroad. For instance, in his famous speech on 4 June—"we shall fight on the beaches"—he assured the Commons and the world that in the unlikely event that Britain fell, the Empire would fight on, guarded by the Royal Navy, until the New World came to the aid of the Old. The following day, however, in a message to the Canadian premier, which he rightly expected would be passed on to Roosevelt, Churchill warned:

We must be careful not to let Americans view too complacently the prospect of a British collapse out of which they would get the British fleet and the guardianship of the British Empire, minus Great Britain. If . . . America continued neutral, and we were overpowered I cannot tell what policy might be adopted by a pro-German administration such as would undoubtedly be set up.[64]

For the most part Lothian emulated Churchill's delicate balancing act. In public he stressed Britain's confident determination and reserved his warnings about the fleet for the Administration and small groups of opinion-makers.[65] However, he became increasingly alarmed at the Americans' apparent complacency about the fleet, fearing indeed that this might have been strengthened by Churchill's words on 4 June.[66] By the middle of June, as the French neared surrender and an invasion of Britain appeared imminent, Lothian believed that the Administration ought to speak out publicly. He told the Foreign Office on 16 June, after a long talk with Roosevelt and Secretary of State Cordell Hull the previous day:

My impression is that the United States Government is quite clear that it can do nothing beyond sending supplies as quickly as possible to help France and ourselves in the present juncture but that it has not yet faced the fact that the only way in which it can save itself from being confronted by totalitarian navies and air forces three or four times as powerful as its own in the near future is by setting the situation in all its stark brutality in front of Congress without delaying and inviting it to go to war with all its resources in the hope of saving Britain and France while there is still time.[67]

But both Roosevelt and Hull were adamant that for the president to do this would be to commit political suicide. On 17 June Lothian suggested that they should at least make a full statement to Congress about the gravity of the naval situation and the consequences for the United States of Britain's defeat, in order to bring home to the American public that

---

[64] WSC to Mackenzie King, 5 June 1940, PREM 4/43B/1, pp. 299–300A. On a draft (p. 306) Churchill annotated, presumably for the benefit of future historians: "Probably be seen by President Roosevelt. I hope." The text of his 4 June speech is in *Winston S. Churchill: His Complete Speeches, 1897–1963*, ed. Robert Rhodes James, 6: 6225–6231.

[65] E.g., Breckinridge Long, MS. diary, 21 May 1940 (LC).

[66] PL to FO and WSC, tel 932, 8 June 1940, FO 371/24239, A3316/131/45.

[67] PL to FO, tel. 1007, 16 June 1940, FO 371/24311, C7294/65/17.

assistance to Britain was the best line of defense. Both were noncommittal.[68]

Lothian therefore decided to take matters into his own hands. He took advantage of a speech he was giving at Yale on 19 June to correct the impression that might have been given by Churchill's remarks on June 4 and to warn Americans bluntly of their strategic situation.[69] He told his audience not to build their defenses on the expectation that, whatever happened to Britain, its fleet would be available to defend North America. That, he said, might well prove "an illusion," for two reasons. First, the Royal Navy was far more effective in controlling the exits from Europe into the Atlantic, as it had done during the nineteenth century to America's great benefit, than in trying to patrol a vast seaboard on the other side of the ocean. Second, most of the fleet would probably be lost in defending Britain. Only when it had done all it could to hold the home islands would it leave for overseas ports. Most of the ships would go to the Empire, leaving few for the United States, even assuming that the British were willing to entrust them to a neutral power. Lothian stressed that he was not pessimistic about the outcome of the battle of Britain, nor was he trying to tell Americans their business. He said he was simply concerned that, if the worst happened, Americans did not ask why they had not been informed of these strategic verities, so that they could decide their own policy in time.

Lothian believed that this speech put "the issue to the United States as bluntly as it is possible for any Ambassador to do."[70] His remarks were widely reported and British leaders were full of praise.[71] But in retrospect it would seem that Lothian had gone too far; he did not fully appreciate the ramifications of his direct warning. It was not so much that Roosevelt himself was unsettled by Britain's scare-tactics about surrendering the fleet. During June he gradually came to the conclusion that they were bluffing and that Churchill's words on 4 June, about the fleet going to the Empire if Britain proved untenable, represented a true statement of his intentions.[72] What mattered was the effect of Lothian's *public* comments on the political credibility of the president's diplomacy.

For one thing, Lothian's Yale speech made it harder for Roosevelt to maintain the existing division of labor between the U.S. fleet in the Pacific and the British in the Atlantic. On 17 June, when the ambassador urged Roosevelt to speak out about the naval consequences for America if Britain fell, the president pointed out that if such a statement went too far "it might produce a demand for the removal of the American fleet from the Pacific to the Atlantic which would have disastrous effects in the Pacific

---

[68] PL to FO, tel. 1019, 17 June 1940, FO 371/24240, A3582/131/45.

[69] As he explained in PL to FO, tel. 1080, 22 June 1940, FO 371/24246, A3007/301/45. The text is in *American Speeches*, pp. 104–109.

[70] PL to WSC, tel. 1 July 1940, LP 399: 614.

[71] WSC to PL, tel. 1515, 14 July 1940 and Halifax to PL, 15 July, A3007.

[72] Moffat diary, 10 June and 5 July 1940.

Ocean."[73] Lothian, of course, was fully aware in principle of the United States fleet's value as a deterrent against Japan. What he apparently did not appreciate at this date was that Roosevelt was already under strong pressure from some senior State Department officials and from the Army and Navy chiefs to abandon the Pacific and move most of the fleet back through the Panama Canal to defend the Atlantic coast.[74] Lothian and the Embassy began to realize the extent of this pressure on 20 June, but that was the day after he had made his Yale speech.[75] The immediate crisis was solved in early July by the British action to neutralize the French fleet—which was taken with the president's full knowledge and support[76]—but Lothian's remarks probably had a further effect on Roosevelt's diplomacy. They may well have made him more cautious about providing the destroyers that Britain continued to request. Lothian had hoped to show Americans that Britain was their first and only line of defense and that she must therefore be helped. The president believed that large-scale assistance to Britain, particularly the transfer of destroyers, was only possible with congressional approval, given with near unanimity. Significant criticism, even from a handful of determined senators, could undermine the domestic consensus on which policy must be based. Consequently, a *public* statement by the British ambassador that the British fleet might not come to the U.S.A. made it politically more difficult to reinforce that fleet with United States destroyers. If Britain fell, those destroyers might simply be surrendered to Hitler, for use against the United States. The Canadian premier, in close touch with Roosevelt throughout the summer, was probably right when he suggested later that Lothian's Yale speech was one reason why the president was so insistent in August that, before the destroyers could be transferred, Churchill must clarify the position by stating that his 4 June words about the fleet fighting on if necessary overseas were indeed official British policy.[77]

It seems, then, that Lothian may have gone too far in his efforts to "educate" American opinion. He was probably carried away by his anxiety about Britain's position. That anxiety is, in fact, a fundamental feature of Lothian's thinking during the summer of 1940 and it helps explain both his successes and mistakes in handling the complex of negotiations that led up to the Destroyers Deal. It has been suggested that Lothian favored an early peace with Hitler after France had fallen. The evidence for this is inconclusive, and such an assumption is probably incorrect, but Lothian did urge Halifax on 22 July at least to find out Hitler's peace terms before

---

[73] Tel. cited in note 68.

[74] Cf. e.g. *The War Diary of Breckinridge Long: Selections from the War Years, 1939–1944*, ed. Fred L. Israel, 16 June 1940, p. 107; Mark S. Watson, *Chief of Staff: Prewar Plans and Preparations*, p. 111.

[75] Cf. PL to FO, tel. 1057 and Casey to Canberra, copy, both 20 June 1940, FO 371/24725, F3450/23/23.

[76] PL to FO, tel. 1206, 2 July 1940, FO 371/24321, C7553/839/17; cf. PL to FDR, 4 July, PSF 50: GB reports.

[77] As stated in Sir Gerald Campbell to Sir Eric Machtig, 17 August 1940, PREM 3/464/3, p. 83.

closing the door on negotiation and condemning humanity to further slaughter.[78] Moreover, it is clear that in mid-summer Lothian was far from certain that the British Isles could survive Hitler's onslaught. From comments he made after the fall of France his staff judged that he considered evacuation of the government and fleet to Canada a real possibility.[79] Indeed on 19 June Lothian went so far as to suggest to the Foreign Office that, in case the worst happened, specifications of types of ammunition and all essential drawings should be sent immediately to Canada so that British vessels could easily be serviced and repaired.[80] It should be noted, however, that Lothian's pessimism was neither unqualified nor unrelieved. He felt that his worse fears would be realized if the United States failed to give quick and massive support, particularly in the form of destroyers. His moments of deepest gloom coincided with bouts of acute depression about America. One such period was in the second half of June, with Britain alone and the Administration unwilling to speak or act. This led him to make his Yale speech. The other period was at the beginning of August, when, as we shall see in a moment, renewed pessimism acted as a catalyst for a series of actions Lothian took in order to get a destroyers deal off the ground.

Joseph Lash has suggested that Lothian's pessimism colored his reporting of Roosevelt's policy, that he tended to project on to the president

---

[78] Cf. Lash, *Roosevelt and Churchill*, p. 200. The main source for this claim is a note in Harold Nicolson's diary for 22 July 1940: "Philip Lothian telephones wildly from Washington this evening begging Halifax not to say anything in his broadcast tonight which might close the door to peace. Lothian claims that he knows the German peace-terms and that they are most satisfactory." (Nicolson, *Diaries and Letters*, 2: 104.) It is most unlikely that Nicolson knew anything of this directly. He was only a junior minister at the Ministry of Information and was presumably only relating Whitehall or Clubland gossip.

The actual circumstances seem to be as follows: On 19 July Lothian reported that he had been approached by the German chargé d'affaires in Washington through a Quaker intermediary to say that, if he wanted, the chargé could obtain Berlin's present peace terms. Lothian was instructed to make no reply. On 22 July he did speak on the phone with Halifax, whose note of the conversation reads as follows: "Another approach through the same source—Lord Lothian could get the information as to what he means if we want it. There is a certain amount of, not official, feeling. We ought to find out what Hitler means before condemning the world to 1,000,000 casualties." (FO 371/24407, p. 71, C7377/89/18.) Lothian told the FO that the initial overture had come from the German side and that on 19 July the Quaker intermediary, Malcolm Lovell, had only spoken with his Counsellor, Nevile Butler. But Lovell claimed that he had talked with Lothian himself who said that he longed for peace if terms could be devised that "a proud and unconquered nation" could accept. Cf. Lothian to FO, tel. 1417, 19 July 1940, FO 371/24408, C8015/89/18, with Laurence Thompson, *1940: Year of Legend, Year of History*, pp. 9, 159–65, based on Lovell's contemporary record of events. The German documents have not survived—cf. *Documents on German Foreign Policy, 1918–1945*, series D, vol. XI, p. 42. The British official historian argues that German claims that Lothian initiated the contacts—cf. *The Memoirs of Ernst von Weizsäcker*, tr. John Andrews, pp. 237–8—were part of an attempt to convince the U.S.A. that she would be unwise to trust Britain's resolution (Woodward, *British Foreign Policy*, II, 192, note 1). The German line is developed by Bernd Martin, *Friedensinitiativen und Machtpolitik im Zweiten Weltkrieg, 1939–1942*, pp. 298–9, 317–21, who prefers Lovell's account to that of Lothian.

[79] Morgan, interview, 31 July 1977, reconstructing the conclusion reached by himself and John Wheeler-Bennett.

[80] PL to FO, tel. 1032, 19 June 1940, PREM 3/476/10, p. 544.

his own sense of discouragement.[81] But it is clear that Roosevelt's limited support for Britain that summer was due not merely to the United States' own military weakness and to the constraints of domestic politics, but in part to his doubts about whether Britain could survive alone as America's front line. A brief review of the evidence will demonstrate this. When the German offensive began in May, Roosevelt hinted to close associates that the United States might be in the war by mid-August.[82] But that was before the disastrous collapse of the Western Front became apparent. By late May, with the British army apparently inextricably trapped in Flanders, Roosevelt anticipated an early French surrender, "doubted if England would be able to bear up" against the Lutfwaffe's five to one superiority and feared that the British would accept a German peace offer involving the surrender of the fleet.[83] With the "miracle of Dunkirk," the president's hopes partially revived. He intensified his efforts to secure the release of United States rifles, ammunition, and aircraft for sale to Britain and France and gave an inspiring statement of his dual policy of rearmament and aid to "the opponents of force" in his Charlottesville speech on 10 June. Three days later he told his planners to work on the hypothesis that Britain would still be intact by the end of the year, and on 17 June, as the French surrendered, he said that Britain should be given the same help as had been given to Britain and France.[84] But, for all this, Roosevelt did little to assist Britain until the beginning of August. Of course, the United States had little surplus equipment available and its sale was limited by new congressional legislation in late June. And Roosevelt, a lame-duck president trying to engineer an unprecedented third term, was in a delicate political position. But Lothian judged on 27 June that the president had been affected by the "wave of pessimism" about Britain's chances of survival that passed over the United States after the French collapse. Other close observers of the president at this time offer similar testimony.[85]

---

[81] Lash, *Roosevelt and Churchill*, p. 167. Like Gloria J. Barron, *Leadership in Crisis: FDR and the Path to Intervention*, e.g. pp. 61–62, Lash presents Roosevelt as unswerving in his belief that Britain would survive.

[82] On the evening of 16 May Roosevelt approved a further French aircraft order. "Work it out in swap," he told Morgenthau, meaning that the French should be allowed to buy planes currently in service with the Army Air Corps, while releasing for the United States their own orders scheduled for delivery in July. Then, according to Morgenthau: "He said after all we will not be in it for *60 or 90 days*." (MPD, 3: 545; emphasis in original.)

[83] Mackenzie King, Diary, memo "Re: Interviews with President Roosevelt," dated 27 May 1940 quoting report of the Canadian diplomat, Hugh Keenleyside, about his talk with Roosevelt and Hull on 25 May.

[84] Maurice Matloff and Edwin M. Snell, *Strategic Planning for Coalition Warfare, 1941–1942*, pp. 13–14; MPD 3: 585, 17 June 1940.

[85] PL to FO, tel. 1135, 27 June 1940, PREM 3/476/10, p. 531. See also Thomas W. Lamont to PL, Aug. 7, 1940 (Lamont papers, Harvard Business School, 105–12), in which he refers to the lack of confidence in Britain and says: "I believe that even F.D.R. has been affected by such talk." For a similar view a month earlier see Lamont to Lady Astor, 10 July, p. 2 (ibid., 82–6). Jim Farley, Roosevelt's erstwhile campaign manager, claims that on 7 July the president told him that Britain's chances were "about one in three." (James A. Farley, *Jim Farley's Story: The Roosevelt Years*, pp. 244–45, 253.) In late July William Allen White believed that, since winning the third-term nomination, Roosevelt "had, as it were, lost his cud." (Walter Johnson, *The Battle against Isolation*, p. 100).

Such doubts were hardly surprising, if one eschews the wisdom of hindsight. Whatever Roosevelt said on 17 June, the question of backing Britain alone was clearly very different from that of helping Britain and France maintain a Western front on the continent. And there was much truth in the arguments of such as Ambassador Kennedy that Britain's diplomatic and military record over the previous few years hardly recommended her as a reliable ally. Aside from all the political and legal problems, until Britain's position seemed more certain, Roosevelt felt it was unwise to fritter away America's scarce resources, especially destroyers, which might subsequently fall into Hitler's hands and be used against the United States.[86] It was not until August that he became more confident that Britain would pull through, that she could survive alone as America's front line. This was an essential pre-condition for supplying the destroyers.

To return to Lothian, we have seen that anxiety about Britain's position led him, unlike Churchill, to overstate his warnings about the British fleet, but, in further contrast to the Prime Minister, Lothian believed in using the carrot as well as the stick in his efforts to secure American help. Throughout the summer he repeatedly urged Britain to woo the United States with attractive offers of cooperation. While of greater immediate benefit to the United States than to Britain, such cooperation would encourage reciprocal generosity and promote that spirit of Anglo-American amity which Lothian believed was essential for the future of the world. Churchill, however, was hesitant. He remained suspicious of American intentions and preferred to tailor British concessions to tangible evidence of United States help. This tactical difference recurred throughout the summer. For example, Churchill was slow to take up Roosevelt's proposal in mid-June for staff conversations. This had been elicited after sustained pressure from Lothian, but the Prime Minister feared that any talks "would turn almost entirely on the American side upon the transfer of the British fleet to trans-Atlantic bases."[87] Such suspicions were understandable in view of Roosevelt's repeated reminders about the fleet, most recently restated in a forceful letter of 17 June from the Canadian premier. Churchill would have been even more alarmed had he known that secretly Lothian had been using the idea of contingency planning for moving the fleet as bait to entice the United States into conversations.[88] Only after strong pressure from Halifax did Churchill agree to go ahead. Similarly, Churchill was reluctant to make a spontaneous offer to the U.S.A. of Britain's military secrets. Although agreeing in principle on 30 June, after repeated urging by Lothian, the Foreign Office, and the service departments, the premier

---

[86] Ickes, *Secret Diary* 3: 199–200, 233. FDR to Ickes, 6 July 1940, OF 4044: "I always have to think of the possibility that if these destroyers were sold to Great Britain and if, thereupon, Great Britain should be overwhelmed by Germany, they might fall into the hands of the Germans and be used against us."

[87] WSC to Halifax, 24 June 1940, A3582.

[88] As pointed out in Leutze, *Bargaining for Supremacy*, p. 132. Cf. PL to FO, tel. 1105, 24 June 1940, A3582 on a conversation with Hull, with Hull's record of same talk in Hull papers, 58/213 (LC).

still held back in practice. In part this reflected his obession with secrecy. But he was also concerned with tactical considerations. As he minuted on 17 July: "Are we going to throw all our secrets into the American lap; and see what they give us in exchange? If so, I am against it. . . . Generally speaking, I am not in a hurry to give our secrets until the United States is much nearer war than she is now."[89] Only on 8 August, when it was clear that Roosevelt was serious about a destroyers deal, did Churchill give his permission for a special technical mission to leave for America.

The most striking instance of this difference over tactics between Lothian and the Foreign Office on the one hand and Churchill on the other is to be found in their respective attitudes to the question of offering America bases in British possessions. Britain's Caribbean islands had long been an irritant in Anglo-American relations, but they assumed a new importance in the spring of 1940 with the German successes in Europe. United States bases on these islands would greatly strengthen the defenses of the Panama Canal and the East Coast. They would also help prevent these colonies falling into German hands as the result of a European peace settlement. Lothian was well aware of the concern about the islands within the Administration and Congress. He repeatedly urged his government to make a spontaneous offer of facilities, to preempt a possible United States takeover of the islands and also promote goodwill and cooperation. His first proposal to this effect was sent on 25 May, when London was preoccupied with the Dunkirk evacuation and bitter at the lack of American help. Although the Foreign Office and chiefs of staff supported Lothian, Churchill and the Admiralty, anxious for United States destroyers, felt no offer should be made except as part of a deal from which Britain benefited as well. The Colonial and Dominions Offices also feared that bases would be the first step to United States domination in the Caribbean. The matter therefore lapsed until 23 June, when Lothian made a more limited suggestion to offer the United States facilities on three Caribbean possessions. Once again the Foreign Office was enthusiastic, but the Admiralty and the Colonial and Dominion Offices sought a quid pro quo such as destroyers or financial credits. For much of July the matter became bogged down in interdepartmental argument, despite repeated pleas from Lothian. Eventually Foreign Office/American Department forced it out of the morass of bureaucratic politics and it came before the Cabinet on 29 July. While the Colonial Office still feared the thin end of an American imperial wedge, the consensus was that Britain should take up Lothian's limited proposal. The Cabinet therefore agreed to offer Pan American Airways, as agents for the United States Government, leases of land to build a small store and radio station on Trinidad, and airfields in British Guiana and Jamaica, as well as giving the United States landing rights for military aircraft in those three colonies.[90]

---

[89] WSC to Ismay, 17 July 1940, PREM 3/475/1, pp. 33–34.
[90] See esp. FO 371/24255, A3297/2961/45 and FO 371/24256, A3600/2961/45; also CAB 65/7, WM (40) 141/9 and 146/14 and CAB 65/8, WM (40) 214/4.

Ostensibly the Cabinet had accepted the argument of Lothian and Foreign Office/American Department that a spontaneous offer would facil-
itate goodwill and cooperation. In fact, however, the Cabinet's decision
was tied very closely to Britain's renewed pressure for United States destroyers. Once more Lothian guided policy here. On 22 July he cabled
that, with the conventions over and Roosevelt's nomination secured,
American attention was turning again to the war and to the question of
how to help Britain. In several messages over the next few days he focused
the government's thinking once more on the question of destroyers. Foreign Office officials now urged Churchill to send Roosevelt himself a new
plea.[91] Churchill began drafting but was uncertain about the rightness of
this step. The two leaders had not been in touch for six weeks, apart from
one peripheral message from Churchill, and the premier had been deterred
from cabling about destroyers in early July because Ambassador Kennedy
warned against further rhetorical appeals which might seem like emotional
blackmail.[92] On 30 July, however, Lothian told Churchill: "Strong pressure
is being brought on the President to reconsider possibility of supplying
us with destroyers. Now is the moment to send him most moving statement of our needs and dangers in respect of destroyers and flying boats
you can, if you have not already done so." This decided Churchill. Now
was the time "to plug it in," he told Halifax. In a long telegram to the
president on 31 July the Prime Minister set out Britain's naval predicament
in detail, listed her recent destroyer losses and explained that fifty United
States destroyers could tide the Royal Navy over the next few critical
months, thereby possibly deciding "the whole fate of the war." On 2
August, after delay caused by continued Colonial Office obstruction, the
Cabinet's 29 July limited offer of bases was conveyed to Lothian.[93] The
relation between the two British initiatives was not coincidence.

When Lothian spoke in his 30 July cable about strong pressure being
brought to bear upon the president, he knew what he was talking about.
In addition to urging London to act on the destroyers and the bases, he
had been in touch for several weeks with groups close to Roosevelt who
advocated the speedy transfer of destroyers to Britain. Of these the most
important were the Cabinet "hawks"—Henry Morgenthau (Treasury),
Frank Knox (Navy), Henry Stimson (War), and Harold Ickes (Interior)—
who together were to promote several important foreign policy initiatives
in the next few months. In the matter of destroyers the leading spirit was
Knox, the newly-appointed Navy secretary, who had long sought acqui-
sition or access to British bases in the Caribbean. Lothian had been in
touch with Knox since the latter's appointment in late June, reminding
him of the need for destroyers and relaying to London Knox's interest in

---

[91] See A 3582, esp. PL tels. 1456, 1492, 1507, 22, 25 and 26 July; Vansittart to WSC,
23 July, PREM 3/462/2-3, p. 159.
[92] See PREM 3/462/2-3, pp. 151-58 and Kennedy to Hull, tel. 2001, 5 July 1940, *Foreign
Relations of the United States* (FRUS), 1940, 3: 56.
[93] A3582, esp. PL to WSC, tel. 1553, 30 July; WSC to Halifax, 30 July; WSC to FDR,
31 July; FO to PL, tel. 1759, 2 August 1940.

bases.[94] In late July with the conventions over, Knox renewed his pressure on the president. On the evening of 1 August he found Lothian "almost tearful in his pleas for help and help quickly."[95] In response Knox suggested the idea of a destroyers-bases deal. The following day he concerted tactics with Stimson and Ickes (Morgenthau was away) for the afternoon's Cabinet meeting, and undoubtedly their pressure helped push Roosevelt into action. But the United States Cabinet believed that an assurance about the Royal Navy would be far more important than the bases in convincing Congress that the arrangement would enhance United States security. "The feeling was that the one preoccupying thought on the Hill is what may happen to the British Navy," noted Ickes in his diary record of the meeting.[96] Although Lothian was not mentioned by name, it seems likely that his unsettling Yale speech was much in the Cabinet's mind.

On 3 August Roosevelt saw Lothian. He explained the idea of trading fifty or sixty destroyers for an assurance about the fleet and sites for bases in the Western Hemisphere. At this stage Roosevelt was still exploring its feasibility. But over the next ten days, as his confidence about Britain increased and assurances of tacit Republican support were forthcoming, he became committed to acting. His path was simplified by a convenient legal opinion that he could proceed by his much-favored device of an executive agreement rather than by legislation. The main obstacle now was Churchill. Having for months advocated a quid pro quo approach to Anglo-American cooperation and having accepted in early August the idea of a limited bases-destroyers deal, the Prime Minister now backed away as the scope of the proposed destroyers-bases-assurance deal became apparent. He feared that it would be politically unacceptable in Britain. Instead of the limited facilities in three British colonies that the Cabinet had agreed to offer on 29 July, the United States now wanted full bases on seven sites. Churchill was willing to accept this, but insisted that, since the deal was clearly to the United States' benefit, the two elements should not be explicitly related and should be treated as mutual gifts, offered in a spirit of amity and cooperation. He felt that an assurance about the fleet was quite out of the question, partly because it gave the United States too much but mainly because he feared that further public mention of the matter would unsettle domestic morale at a crucial moment. After protracted negotiation, the bases were divided. Two were presented as a gift, the rest as quid pro quo for the destroyers. On the fleet assurance, the Administration eventually secured what it wanted. By incremental diplomacy it got Churchill to reiterate his 4 June statement in the form of an *aide-mémoire*. It then persuaded him that this should be published.[97]

---

[94] Cf. Knox to PL, 20 June 1940, LP 402: 153 and PL to FO, tel. 1307, 10 July, A3297.

[95] Ickes, *Secret Diary*, 3: 283.

[96] Ibid., p. 292. For other accounts of the meeting and of the background to it see Henry L. Stimson diary, 30: 55–58 (Sterling Library, Yale University) and FDR's memo of 2 August in *FRUS*, 1940, 3: 58–59.

[97] For discussion see books cited in note 59. (An eighth site, on Antigua, was added late in the negotiations.)

Lothian had little sympathy with Churchill's objections. For months he had been pressing the Administration on one hand for destroyers and his own government on the other for an offer of bases. To couple the two in this way would solve United States political problems, symbolize transatlantic ties and lay the foundation for that sharing of naval responsibilities which Lothian believed was essential for world peace. Furthermore, in early August the ambassador was suffering from one of his periodic bouts of depression. The "almost tearful" pleas to Knox on 1 August were not contrived. Overworked, troubled by rheumatism and by the Washington heat, Lothian was again pessimistic about Britain's chances of survival.[98] He was also convinced that the destroyers were essential. By contrast, Churchill, especially when peeved at the Americans, was ready to assert that Britain could still get through the crucial remainder of 1940 without them.[99]

This desperate sense of urgency affected Lothian's handling of the diplomatic negotiations throughout August, and exacerbated his customary impatience with detail. On the morning of 3 August, for instance, when Roosevelt proposed the destroyers-bases-assurance idea, Lothian seized on it enthusiastically. Although cautious about the assurance, he told Roosevelt that he had been authorized to say that the naval and air facilities would be made available as soon as Britain got the destroyers. At this stage, no such authorization had been given. Lothian either confused certain telegrams or else anticipated Britain's approval of a simple destroyers-bases transaction, which arrived later that day.[100] For a time Lothian also aggravated Churchill's anger about the fleet assurance. Throughout the summer the ambassador had been prone to rather hasty drafting of telegrams, though perhaps this is understandable in view of the pressure of work and urgency of events. At any rate, the careless construction and lack of punctuation in a telegram from Lothian on 5 August led Churchill to understand that Roosevelt wanted the right to decide when the fleet should leave British waters. It took several days to clear up the misun-

---

[98] See PL to Lady Astor, 7 August, Nancy Astor papers, 4/59 (Reading University Library, MS. 1416/1); Goodhart, *Fifty ships*, p. 157; Leutze, *Bargaining for Supremacy*, p. 286, n. 70.

[99] See Cadogan, note, 23 August and WSC to FDR, tel. 2036, 25 August, FO 371/24259, A3917/3742/45.

[100] The Cabinet's decision of 29 July was finally communicated to Lothian in FO tel. 1759, 2 August, 4:10 p.m., A3582. After Lothian had reported—following his 1 August conversation with Knox—that the United States was likely to propose destroyers-bases deal (tel. 1579, 2 August, 1:53 a.m., A3582), Churchill sent his approval in tel. 1776, 3 August, 11:50 p.m., A3600. Clearly this could not have arrived before Lothian's talk with Roosevelt on the morning of 3 August, which he reported in tel. 1606, 4 August, 1:23 a.m., FO 371/24241, A3670/131/45. The contents of PL to FO, tel. 1591, 3 August, 1:6 a.m., A3600, suggests that PL may have misread tel. 1759 as an answer to his tel. 1579 about a destroyers-bases deal. Or he may have simply anticipated WSC's approval, since, as I have shown, the bases offer of 29 July was implicitly tied very closely to Cabinet expectations about destroyers. Lothian's mistake was therefore far less grave than is implied in Leutze, *Bargaining of Supremacy*, pp. 107–111 where he seems to suggest that Lothian's linkage of the destroyers and bases forced Britain into a deal. In my judgment, this is to neglect the connection which was already in London's mind in late July, and to overlook the approval for a destroyers-bases deal given in tel. 1776.

derstanding and mollify the aggrieved Prime Minister.[101] Lothian's sense of urgency also led him to reverse his own attitude to the fleet assurance. On 5 July he had suggested that, if asked, formal assurance should be given that if Britain were on the point of collapse and if the United States had entered the war, then the fleet would cross the Atlantic to American waters. He argued that the United States could only be moved to war if convinced that this was the only way to make sure of the British fleet. Churchill entirely agreed.[102] But when the deal was mooted in August, it was Churchill who stuck to their agreed position. Lothian was quite ready to give the Administration the assurance it wanted, rather than tying the movement of the Royal Navy to United States entry into the war. While the Prime Minister still wanted to retain the fleet as a bargaining counter, Lothian was ready to play that card to get the destroyers he considered vital.

Lothian's determination to conclude the deal as quickly as possible also affected his conduct of the final stages of the negotiations. Although for convenience historians refer to the "destroyers deal," it should be remembered that the British had also been asking for twenty motor torpedo boats (MTBs), five heavy bombers, five flying boats and 250,000 rifles with ammunition. Roosevelt intended to include MTBs, planes and probably rifles in the deal, and this was made clear in mid-August.[103] Yet the final United States note mentioned only destroyers, and it was not until the following spring, after complex legal and political difficulties, that the whole transaction was completed. It has been suggested that Lothian simply overlooked the omission in the final United States note.[104] While that is quite untrue, Lothian must bear part of the blame for the confusion, as a brief account will show. Part of the problem was that in late August Stimson and Welles, who had been in charge of the negotiations during August, left Washington for vacations, handing matters back to Hull who had been away since the beginning of the month. They did not make it sufficiently clear, however, what had been agreed to. This later became the "official" Administration explanation.[105] But it would seem that the president was partly responsible. As happened on other occasions, he was rather casual about tying together the tangled threads of a negotiation.[106]

---

[101] See A3670. The ambiguous sentence in PL's tel. 1616, 5 August read: "All you have to do at the moment is to inform me privately that His Majesty's Government is willing to make a declaration to the effect that His Majesty's Government is determined that the British fleet will go on fighting for the Empire even if it is compelled to evacuate Great Britain if and when the President asks for it."

[102] PL to WSC, tel. 1244, 5 July and WSC to PL, tel. 1646, 24 July 1940, PREM 3/462/2–3, pp. 153, 149.

[103] FDR to WSC 14 August 1940, PREM 3/463/1, pp. 156–158; Stimson, diary, 17 August; Mackenzie King to WSC, 18 August, PREM 3/464/3, p. 104.

[104] William L. Langer and S. Everett Gleason, *The Challenge to Isolation, 1937–1940,* p. 769.

[105] E.g., Stimson to Hull, 14 September, and Hull, memo of lunch with FDR and PL, 16 September, Hull papers, 48/138 and 58/213.

[106] FDR to Hull, 2 September 1940, Hull papers, 48/138 stating that he had "carefully read" the final exchange of notes and given his "full and cordial approval." Cf. John Morton Blum, *From the Morgenthau Diaries,* 2: 181–188.

Hull, too, was somewhat negligent. There was plenty of evidence in the papers he was given to show that more than the destroyers were intended in the proposed transaction.[107] Lothian seems to have made two mistakes. He tended to use the word "destroyers" as a shorthand, without continually referring to all Britain's desiderata.[108] More important, he misled London about Washington's attitude. Late on 27 August, when Hull's misapprehension came to light, the secretary said that the other items could not be considered part of the deal for legal reasons. But Lothian told the Foreign Office: "Mr Hull begged me to assure you that the question of transfer of other desiderata, i.e. motor torpedo boats, flying boats and rifles, would be dealt with in the same spirit that the President has shown hitherto and at the earliest possible moment."[109] London took this to mean that the other items were part of the deal, although they would be handled separately for political and legal reasons, and agreed to the exchange of notes on that basis. When Lothian told Hull of this, the secretary immediately insisted that no promise about the other items must be inferred and that before any agreement was signed Lothian must make this quite clear to London. Lothian assured Hull he would, but there is no evidence that he did so.[110]

Although somewhat careless in finalizing the diplomatic negotiations, Lothian played an invaluable part during August in helping "sell" the deal to the American public. Since late June, he and members of his staff, particularly John Foster, had been in touch with pro-British pressure groups, notably the William Allen White Committee and the more extreme Century Group.[111] On 22 July Lothian gave an effective NBC radio interview in which he dealt adroitly with questions about his record in the 1930s, asserted Britain's determination to win through, and stressed her prime need for "forty or a hundred" destroyers and MTBs.[112] Largely because of this, Lothian was approached by the Century Group for a full statement of Britain's situation and needs, as the basis for a new campaign

---

[107] See Hull papers 47/137.

[108] E.g. PL to Hull, 25 August 1940, Hull papers, 58/213.

[109] PL to FO, tel. 1857, 28 August 1940, FO 371/24259, A3980/3742/45. According to Hull's recollection of the meeting: "I added that all I could say about the other items was to express the opinion that this Government would manifest the same spirit in the future that it had in the past with respect to supplying implements of war." (Hull, memo., 16 September, p. 6; cf. memo of 28 August in Hull papers 58/213.)

[110] FO to PL, tel. 2080, 29 August, A3980; Hull, memo 16 September, pp. 6–7. After protracted negotiations, the British gradually secured most of their desiderata by the spring of 1941.

[111] E.g. PL to William Allen White, 29 June 1940, White papers (LC), C-344; and correspondence with Henry P. Van Dusen, July 1940, LP 405: 517–521. For further background see LP 516; Langer and Gleason, Challenge to Isolation, pp. 746–748 and Mark Lincoln Chadwin, The Warhawks: American Interventionists before Pearl Harbour, esp. pp. 41–42 and 74–108. In reconstructing these events I have benefited from talking with Francis P. Miller and Helen Hill Miller, Washington, D.C., 27 April 1977.

[112] For the press release PL altered the figure to simply "a hundred"—cf. LP 403: 264 and 405: 53. The slightly amended text is printed in American Speeches, pp. 110–115. In FO/A, Perowne entered his ritual protest about Lothian's language, but he was firmly overruled by his superiors. (FO 371/24246, A3732/301/45.)

to secure release of the destroyers. On 25 July Lothian cabled London for the information. He mentioned the reason in vague terms, but by referring to a request from "authoritative quarters" he implied that he was asking on behalf of the administration. Two days later Churchill sent back an Admiralty memo explaining in detail Britain's needs and setting them in the context of the overall strategic situation. The memo stated that in 1918 Britain had 433 destroyers in service and in September 1939, 176, of which 133 were in home waters. By mid-June 1940, however, the latter figures had been reduced to 68 serviceable destroyers, with the prospect of no more than ten new ones in the next four months. Since June, France had surrendered, leaving Britain to patrol both the Atlantic and the Mediterranean at a time when Italy had entered the war and Germany controlled the Baltic and the Channel ports.[113]

This was just the sort of presentation that Lothian wanted. He sent copies or versions of it to members of the Century Group, to the White Committee, to Henry Luce, publisher of *Time* and *Life* magazines, and to influential friends such as Norman Davis—without the permission of London.[114] There is little doubt that the British government would have disapproved had it known. As we have seen, Churchill fully shared Whitehall's perennial paranoia about secrecy, and the Foreign Office, although approving of the pressure groups, believed that the government should keep its distance from them for fear of reviving the American phobia about British propaganda. The official British view—as expressed strongly by Churchill on several occasions—was that "only events will serve to turn opinion in America" and that "it would be wiser to leave the President to manage his own public in this matter."[115] But Lothian was sure this calculated risk was justified in view of the urgency of the situation. As he told one old friend and member of the Century Group to whom he sent the memo:

> Please keep the source of this information confidential.
> Provided the use of the substance of it is likely to lead to the need being met I would take a chance on publicity. You may bet that the Germans know the position pretty accurately. The only people who don't are the great American and British publics who are going to get it in the neck because they are never told facts. Why America sits by and watches its own front door being taken while all top people realise that if it is taken this year America itself is doomed, and that it can save that front door for the matter of 100 destroyers or so, is a mystery to me!! No, it is not a mystery because I have dwelt amongst politicians all my life!!!![116]

Lothian was probably justified. In late July and early August, there seemed an unbridgeable gap between the Administration's recognition of

[113] PL to WSC, tel. 1492, 25 July, and WSC to PL, tel. 1705, 27 July 1940, A3582.

[114] See memos in LP 516/4; FO 800/398, US/40/17–18; Norman Davis papers, 40: "Lothian"; and Eichelberger to White, 8 August, White papers, C-341. Embassy staff made use of it in conversations with prominent interventionists (cf. Ickes, *Secret Diary* 3: 282).

[115] Cf. Halifax to Dr. William Paton, 7 August 1940, FO 371/24241, A3768: WSC, minutes to Morrison and to Pound, 5 July and 9 August 1940, PREM 4/25/8, pp. 649, 607.

[116] PL to Whitney Shepardson, 28 July 1940, Shepardson papers, box 7 (FDRL).

America's stake in Britain's survival and the awareness of this by the general public. The basic problem was the lack of hard facts about Britain's destroyers strength. Even informed military commentators and congressmen were quoting figures of 150–200.[117] Such statistics failed to distinguish between the Royal Navy's total nominal complement of destroyers and the number fit for service in home waters around Britain. The latter was the crucial figure in Britain's defense against invasion. And it was this statistic that Lothian's memo provided. Although he usually asked his correspondents not to use the exact figure of 68—apparently to prevent London guessing who had leaked the information—a rough figure of 60 to 70 was usually quoted in material circulated by the Century Group and the White Committee. This information undoubtedly helped to bring home the gravity of Britain's position to opinion leaders in the United States. Moreover, later in August, the two groups set up a joint information service, run by John L. Balderston, to provide material on Britain's needs to selected newspapers outside Washington and New York who lacked easy access to it themselves. Fifty papers, with a total circulation of over 100,000, were on the list. In his first cable, on 24 August, Balderston stated elliptically:

British now have only about sixty destroyers available their home waters and it would be useful print this fact without indicating source. Reason British published figures indicate double this number is because great numbers light ships have been damaged force under water explosions at some distance and British hoped Germans wouldn't find out and now when figures have reached such alarming proportions British unwilling home public learn truth. British now losing hundred thousand tons week merchant shipping by planes and submarines greater part of this loss due lack of destroyers for convoy. Most serious feature these preventable losses not loss ships but loss cargoes and the effect on merchant sailors of lack escorts. Without our help balance of this year until new crop destroyers in service most serious situation will develop which might be fatal even without successful invasion.[118]

By this date, of course, the negotiations for the deal were in their final stages. But the editors were most appreciative of Balderston's material and used it immediately in columns and editorials.[119] It may well have helped establish a favorable mood when the deal was announced on 3 September.

This aspect of Lothian's activities demonstrates again his awareness of how American policy-making operated. We saw in connection with his Phoney War speeches that he appreciated the value of a well-timed, well-

---

[117] E.g. Lord Strathallan, note, no date, [before 10 August], on views of Senator Hale, ranking Republican member of Senate Naval Affairs Commt., FO 115/3421, G46; White Commt., "Notes on Aid to Britain—II," misdated 8 April 1940 [probably 8 August], in Frank P. Graham papers, 1940—198 (Southern Historical Collection, Univ. of N.C., Chapel Hill).

[118] Circular telegram, 24 August, John L. Balderston papers (LC), box 1. For background see Johnson, *Battle against Isolation*, pp. 117–119.

[119] See, e.g., letters to Francis P. Miller from: Robert Choate (Boston *Herald* and *Traveller*), 29 August; Jim Derieux (*The State*, Columbia, S.C.), 5 September; H. B. Elliston (*Christian Science Monitor*), 24 August; Bill Waymark (Des Moines *Register* and *Tribune*), 26 August. Copies in Balderston papers, box 1.

publicized utterance. Like a pebble thrown into a pool, it set in motion ripples of discussion among opinion-leaders and the foreign-policy public. It was also the perfect answer to American phobia about British propaganda—allowing the natural mechanisms of the U.S. media to do Britain's publicity for her. By the summer, moreover, Lothian and his staff also appreciated that Britain would not get American help simply by emotional appeals and warnings. Habitually suspicious of perfidious Albion and its entangling tentacles, Americans had to be convinced by hard facts that assistance was really needed. Lothian's appreciation of the techniques of publicity and the importance of information were to be displayed most outstandingly in his handling of Britain's dollar crisis in the final month of his life.

V. Lothian's Failings: The Far
Eastern Example

B efore examining this last phase of Lothian's ambassadorship, we should explore a little further some of the weaknesses of his diplomatic technique. We have seen that Lothian was a man of erratic moods and that, at times of crisis, he tended to become preoccupied with a single policy goal, to the detriment both of details and of wider considerations. During the Destroyers Deal these weaknesses were not ultimately of great moment. But they were also apparent in Lothian's handling of Far Eastern policy that summer, and there the consequences could have been much graver.

In a letter written in November 1939, Lothian expressed his belief that the Americans were fundamentally right about the Far East, as Britain was right about Europe. By that he meant that only firm measures would undermine the Japanese militarists and prepare the way for an acceptable settlement. This would involve Japan's withdrawal from China and her acknowledgment of Chinese sovereignty.[120] The following summer, however, Lothian changed his tune. Japan had taken advantage of the European crisis to apply new pressure on China and the colonial powers in Asia, and the Roosevelt Administration made it clear to London in late June that it could offer no support, diplomatic or otherwise. In these circumstances Lothian endorsed the Cabinet's decision, taken after insistent Japanese pressure, to close the "Burma Road" into China for a three-month period.[121] This was essentially an attempt to placate Japan in the short-term until the invasion threat had been countered and Britain was in a position to take firmer action. But Lothian seems to have favored more than a tactical concession. Like the British Ambassador in Tokyo, Sir Robert Craigie, he urged the government to explore the possibilities of a proper Far Eastern settlement with Japan. As a basis he suggested guaranteeing Japan access to oil and rubber in return for a generous settlement of the China incident and an agreement by Japan to keep out of the European war and to prevent Germany from moving into the Pacific.[122] Presumably this shift in policy reflected Lothian's deep anxiety after the Fall of France about Britain's capacity to survive. By mid-July he

---

[120] PL to Hoare, 3 November 1939, FO 800/397, US/39/3.

[121] E.g., PL to FO, tel. 1286, 10 July 1940, FO 371/24667, F3568/43/10.

[122] See Craigie to FO, tel. 1068, 23 June, and PL to FO, tels. 1117 and 1138, 26 and 27 June 1940, FO 371/24725, F3432/23/23; and PL to FO, tel. 1247, 5 July FO 371/24666, F3544/43/10.

was less depressed and he swung back to a policy of firmness, with extremely important repercussions. This episode merits further examination.

At this time there was an ominous increase in Japanese oil purchases. The State Department favored imposing limited restrictions, while the Cabinet "hawks," led in this case by Morgenthau, the Treasury secretary, and Stimson, secretary of war, believed that only a complete embargo would make Japan pause. On the evening of 18 July, while this debate was developing, Lothian entertained Knox, Stimson, and Morgenthau at dinner. The discussion was frank. Lothian criticized the lack of United States aircraft production and Stimson hit back by attacking Britain's closure of the Burma Road. The only way to treat Japan, he insisted, was not to give in to her on anything. Stimson's lecture upset Lothian. He pointed out that the United States had offered Britain no support over the road and that the she was still shipping aviation fuel to Japan. Out of the interchanges that followed, a still-angry Lothian made a clear and remarkable proposal. According to Morgenthau:

His suggestion was this. He said, "If you will stop shipping aviation gasoline to Japan," he said, "we will blow up the oil wells in Dutch East Indies so that the Japanese can't come down and get that, because," he said, "we have all felt that if we put too much pressure on Japan they would go down there and take those oil wells."

Well, for the moment my breath was taken away and I asked him—I said, "Do I understand, Mr. Ambassador that if the United States agrees to stop the shipment of aviation gasoline, that the British Empire will simultaneously blow up the oil wells in East India?" "Well," he said, "that is my idea. I can't talk for my Government." But I said, "Would you be willing to propose it?" and he said, "Absolutely."[123]

An excited Morgenthau put the proposal to the president the following day. The United States, he advised, should impose a total embargo on oil exports, ostensibly "in the interest of national defense" but actually aimed at Japan. Britain would obtain her supplies elsewhere and would immediately blow up the oil wells in the Netherlands East Indies.[124]

There is little doubt that, as Morgenthau later told his staff, Lothian had only made his proposal because of his anger at Stimson's needling.[125] As the account just quoted suggests, he began to wriggle as soon as he appreciated the enormity of his proposal, but Morgenthau would not let him off the hook. The next day, in accordance with his promise, Lothian sent London an account of the dinner and of the proposal that was being put to Roosevelt, but he made no mention of his own part in formulating the plan.[126] This deception proved wise, for Whitehall was horrified. Even the Far Eastern Department of the Foreign Office, usually inclined to a firm

---

[123] MD 284: 201–202 (quotation); cf. Stimson diary, 18 July.
[124] Memo for FDR, 19 July 1940, MD 284: 122.
[125] MD 284: 209.
[126] PL to FO, tel. 1425, 19 July 1940, FO 371/24741, F3634/677/23.

line with Japan, and Foreign Office/American Department, committed to keeping in step with the United States, deplored the idea. There were two fundamental objections. First, such action might start a Pacific war. Japan obtained 80 percent of her oil from America. If denied this, she would probably attack the Netherlands East Indies. This would start a war which Britain, still bereft of United States commitments, would have to fight alone, at a time when she was facing imminent invasion herself. Second, the action would severely damage Britain's supplies; she relied on the U.S.A. for certain high-quality oils, especially lubricants, and half the Netherlands East Indies output went to the British Empire. Apparently neither Lothian nor the United States "hawks" properly appreciated these facts about Britain's oil position. Little wonder then, that Churchill minuted that the idea was "most dangerous, and should be immediately put a stop to."[127]

Fortunately for the British, Roosevelt sided with the State Department on this question. While feeling the need for some kind of firm action against Japan, he feared that a total embargo would push her into the Netherlands East Indies, thereby beginning a Far Eastern war at a time when America's primary interest was in reinforcing the British Isles. Consequently, after a tangled bureaucratic battle in which Roosevelt once again was somewhat slipshod in coordinating policy, the Administration applied a ban on only the export of aviation gasoline.[128] Whitehall was relieved and Lothian's part in encouraging what was for Britain a dangerous idea remained undetected.

In the next few months, however, Lothian's advocacy of a tough line against Japan became apparent to the Foreign Office. In September he strongly urged Whitehall to apply pressure on Dutch oil companies not to enter into long-term contracts with Japan. He assured London "on unquestionable authority that Hull is now vehement for resisting Japanese pretensions." Here was the usual problem: would the United States match actions to words if the chips were down? With the prospect of a Pacific war if they pushed Japan too hard, British policymakers could not afford to take chances. Even Foreign Office/American Department believed Lothian was too sanguine, "it would be most unwise to count on U.S. chickens before they are hatched," warned the department's head.[129] And the Foreign Office's petroleum experts, convinced that Lothian could think of nothing except Anglo-American cooperation, believed he had failed to state their policy with proper clarity and firmness to the Administration.[130]

Such criticism was not confined to the Foreign Office's petroleum de-

[127] Ibid., esp. minutes by Clarke and Balfour, 20 July; memo by Kirsch, 21 July; and WSC to Ismay, 21 July 1940.
[128] For discussion see Irvine H. Anderson, Jr., *The Standard-Vacuum Oil Company and United States East Asian Policy, 1933–1941*, esp. pp. 129–138, 142–143 note 41.
[129] PL to FO, tel. 1749, 8 September and Balfour, minute, 12 September 1940, FO 371/25213, W10238/9160/49.
[130] Minute by Steel, 2 October 1940, ibid., W10738.

partment. The Ministry of Economic Warfare believed that Lothian was an inadequate advocate of British policy on the blockade. This ministry was headed by Hugh Dalton, a bureaucratic intriguer and empire-builder on the scale of Harold Ickes in Washington. Dalton was firmly committed to maintaining the integrity of Britain's blockade of Germany and Italy—still officially Whitehall's main weapon for winning the war. Lothian, by contrast, responsive to United States public opinion and to the private views of the president, felt that some modification should be made for propaganda purposes. Specifically, he argued that to head off humanitarian criticism in America, notably from ex-president Hoover, Britain should allow limited quantities of food into Vichy France for distribution to children, under United States auspices.[131] Dalton became increasingly angry with Lothian for failing to urge Britain's policy with sufficient force on the Administration.[132] When Lothian returned to London in October he pressed Roosevelt's and his own views on the Ministry of Economic Warfare, persuasively but without success. The most Dalton would concede was that Lothian's plan would be his second line of defense, if the complete retention of the blockade proved diplomatically impossible.[133] In the New Year, after Lothian's death and in response to a direct appeal from Roosevelt, Churchill was obliged to back down and accept a proposal along the lines Lothian had suggested.[134] But there is little doubt that Dalton and the Foreign Office petroleum experts were right to feel in the autumn of 1940 that, on certain issues, Lothian's sensitivity to the American point of view had begun to impair his effectiveness as an advocate of British policy.

---

[131] E.g., Lord Astor to PL, 26 July, and PL to Astor, 3 September 1940, LP 398: 234–235, 240.

[132] Dalton diary, 31 August, 2 September 1940.

[133] Leith Ross, minute of meeting with PL, 25 October 1940, T188/300; Dalton diary, 24 October.

[134] FDR to WSC, 31 December 1940 and WSC to FDR, 3 January 1941, PREM 3/469, pp. 581–583, 579–580. CAB 65/17, WM 1 (41), 3, 2 January 1941.

VI. The Origins of Lend-Lease: Lothian's Vindication

Autumn 1940 marked a lull both in the war and in Anglo-American diplomacy. By October it seemed unlikely that Hitler would mount an invasion of Britain that year, and Americans turned their attention to the presidential election on 5 November. The time seemed opportune for Lothian to visit Britain. He left Washington on 15 October and returned on 23 November, although he was in Britain for less than four weeks because of long delays at Lisbon. The United States military attaché in London believed that the ambassador had deliberately and cleverly arranged to be out of Washington during the delicate election period,[135] but this does not seem to have been the case. Lothian was simply taking his annual leave, which had been delayed by the successive crises of the previous months.[136] He badly needed a vacation, having had only six days of real holiday since taking up his post.[137] He also wanted to deal with his business affairs. His main reason for the visit, however, was to brief the Foreign Office on American policy and to inform himself about the situation and mood in Britain and about the current state of official policy. After an absence of fourteen months, during which the whole international scene had been revolutionized, renewed personal contact was essential.[138]

The visit proved a great success. Although some in Whitehall, such as Dalton, still had a low opinion of him, they were now in a distinct minority. Many were struck by a profound change in his character and outlook. As Churchill remarked in his memoirs, the crisis had transformed Lothian from an entertaining but detached intellectual into "an earnest, deeply-stirred man . . . primed with every aspect and detail of the American

---

[135] *The London Observer: The Journal of General Raymond E. Lee, 1940–1941,* ed. James Leutze, 3 November 1940, p. 120. Lee may have had in mind the celebrated Sackville-West incident of 1888, when the then British Ambassador was asked to leave after a private letter of his, expressing a preference for Cleveland over Harrison, was published at the height of the election campaign.

[136] PL had asked in April to take leave in July, but this had proved impossible because of the European crisis and the destroyers negotiations. His return to Britain was further delayed by the Axis Tripartite Pact and the reopening of the Burma Road in the early autumn. (See FO 800/324, HXXXVII/67–68 and FO 371/24246, A4354/301/45.) In fact the FO would have preferred him to have been back in Washington for the election. (Scott, minute 2 October 1940, A4354.) This interpretation is confirmed in N. Butler, minute, 15 May 1944, FO 954/30 B, p. 357.

[137] Cf. PL to Percival Witherby 13 October 1940, LP 514: 20.

[138] PL to FO, tel. 2215, 6 October 1940, A4534.

attitude."[139] During his visit Lothian talked at length with Churchill, Halifax, and representatives of most government departments. Their discussions ranged over every aspect of transatlantic relations, from Ireland to the Far East, from propaganda to Latin American trade. Lothian was also anxious to take a long view of relations between the two countries. During his visit he was full of the idea of a standing council in Washington comprising the United States, the American republics and the British Empire, to maintain political and economic cooperation in war and peace. This idea, he said, the president had tossed off before he left Washington.[140] But inevitably the main topics of discussion were the fundamental and interconnected problems of supply, shipping, and finance. How could Britain obtain quick and massive United States support in these areas, without which she had little hope of survival?

For months British policy towards America had waited on the result of the presidential election. The Foreign Office found the United States political process antiquated and confusing. "The Constitution is a disaster," wrote Cadogan, with customary cynicism and succinctness. But they grasped the fundamental point quite clearly; namely, that "for the better part of a year the functioning of the political machine is hampered by election activities and no action can be taken in the political field without very full consideration of its effect on the election."[141] By October 1940 virtually every aspect of Anglo-American relations seemed in suspended animation. On the great question of finance, for instance, Sir Frederick Phillips, a senior Treasury official, had visited Washington in July and had reported that while the ultimate signs were hopeful the Administration would say or do nothing until after the election. The British therefore continued to buy vital supplies, trusting that the United States would help them when their dollar resources were exhausted. Psychologically, this enforced patience had an interesting if not surprising result. November 5 became a magic date for British policymakers. They gradually convinced themselves that as soon as the election was over, the whole situation would change dramatically and United States help would be automatically forthcoming. This would be true, they felt, whoever won, for Wendell Willkie, Roosevelt's opponent, had made clear his support for the Allied cause. Nearly everyone, however, anxiously hoped that Roosevelt would win. "It will be a disaster, I think, for us if he does not," Halifax noted tensely in his diary late in October.[142] For one thing, since the inauguration was not until 20 January, it would be at least six months before a Republican administration began to find its feet. Furthermore, they believed

[139] Churchill, *Second World War*, 2: 490. Cf. Lady Astor to PL, 30 September 1940, on "the way people in England are changing about you." (Astor papers, 4/59.)

[140] Dalton diary, 24 October 1940. These views are developed in "Lord Lothian's last talk at Cliveden" [Nov. 1940], memo, no date, in Altrincham papers, 1941: Astor (Bodleian Library, Oxford, MS. 1005).

[141] Minutes by Cadogan and Scott, 2 April 1940, FO 371/24233, A2286/39/45.

[142] Halifax diary, 27 October 1940 A 7.8.6, p. 321 (Hickleton papers, Borthwick Institute, York).

that Roosevelt, tremendously experienced and fully cognizant of Britain's position, was ready to take the ultimate step. For months Churchill, ever intent on uplifting morale, had been insisting that if Roosevelt was re-elected the United States would quickly enter the war. By early November even habitually cautious officials in the Foreign Office agreed with him.[143] In general, the Foreign Office believed that United States policy would be clear within two weeks of Roosevelt's reelection.

In part, of course, the British were correct. After the election Roosevelt enjoyed greater freedom for political maneuvre and he was able gradually to increase his support for Britain. But British expectations of what Roosevelt would do were clearly exaggerated—for two basic reasons. First, they probably overestimated his readiness to enter the war. To the British he was always at his most bellicose, in order to encourage them to fight on in the expectation of United States help. But Roosevelt spoke with many voices, varying his comments to suit his audience. Robert Dallek, in his study of Roosevelt's foreign policy, judges that it was only in the spring of 1941 that the president decided that the United States would have to enter the war. Earlier authorities tentatively suggested that he did not come to this conclusion until July or September. Even then, the president remained convinced that only after a major "incident" could he go to Congress with any chance of securing the near-unanimous approval necessary for a meaningful declaration of war. And, as Robert Divine suggested some years ago, it remains "quite possible that Roosevelt never fully committed himself to American involvement prior to Pearl Harbor," sensitive not only to isolationist strength but also to the horrific enormity of leading a modern nation into total war.[144]

Second, whatever the accuracy of these speculations, Britain clearly misunderstood Roosevelt's political position. Consciously or not, they were casting United States politics in a British mold, assuming that the election would give Roosevelt a clear-cut "mandate" and the legislative majority with which to execute it. Used to a centralized political system with firm party divisions and tight discipline, they found it hard to grasp the realities of the separation of powers, of loose party authority, and sketchy White House control over the Federal bureaucracy. Nominally the 1940 election would give the president new "overall majorities" of 268 to 167 in the House and 66 to 30 in the Senate.[145] But such figures had little meaning

---

[143] E.g., according to his private secretary, on 1 November Churchill "was sure Roosevelt would win the election by a far greater majority than was supposed, and he believed that America would come into the war." (Sir John Colville, *Footprints in Time*, pp. 144–145.) Cf. North Whitehead, minute, 4 November 1940: "All the underground signs suggest that if Mr. Roosevelt is returned to power tomorrow he will bring in the USA as soon as this proves possible." (FO 371/24243, p. 182).

[144] Robert Dallek, *Franklin D. Roosevelt and American Foreign Policy, 1932–1945*, pp. 285, 530; James MacGregor Burns, *Roosevelt: The Soldier of Freedom*, p. 105; William L. Langer and S. Everett Gleason, *The Undeclared War, 1940–1941*, pp. 458, 735; Robert A. Divine, *Roosevelt and World War II*, p. 48. For fuller discussion see Reynolds, *The Creation of the Anglo-American Alliance 1937–1941*, pp. 204–7, 211–12, 217–20, 288.

[145] Edgar E. Robinson, *They Voted for Roosevelt: The Presidential Vote, 1932–1944*, p. 25.

for Roosevelt's congressional arithmetic. Many conservative Democrats were still deeply suspicious of him, including senior southerners on crucial committees, and Roosevelt was forever fearful that a latter-day "little band of willful men" could obstruct policy and undermine national unity as it had done for Wilson. November 5, therefore, did not relieve the president of the slow and difficult task of gradually creating a foreign-policy consensus among key groups in Congress, the bureaucracy, and among opinion-leaders. As he told one famous interventionist who called on him to clear away the remaining obstructions to helping Britain: "There is no question that the election did not change certain fundamentals in any particular."[146]

Apparently alone among senior British policymakers, Lothian seems to have understood these facts and to have built his policy around them. If anything, he was too dismissive about the election result. He felt that in the long run it would not matter much to Britain who won. The main advantage of a Roosevelt victory, which he anticipated, was simply that it would avoid the dangerous "lame-duck" hiatus before a Republican administration got going.[147] This seems a remarkable judgment. As Lothian's biographer observed, it is difficult to believe that Willkie "could have handled day-to-day questions of tactics with the skill and authority of Franklin Roosevelt."[148] But Lothian's scepticism at least had the merit of being a useful corrective to the exaggerated hopes about Roosevelt entertained by most British leaders. And he also had no expectation of imminent United States entry into the war. At the end of August he told Churchill:

The United States of course is steadily drifting towards war but the constitutional difficulty of getting a Congressional declaration of war unless there is a manifest attack upon American soil or its most vital interests are [sic] such that the United States is likely to find herself fighting under cover in different parts of the world long before formal belligerency is recognised.[149]

Here was a shrewd prediction of Roosevelt's policy in 1941 of limited, undeclared war. In mid-October Lothian expressed the same opinions again. He believed that the United States would remain formally neutral until there had been two further developments in the situation. One was an attack on her vital interests. This would make possible the internal unity without which no declaration of war could be secured. The other

---

[146] FDR to Douglas Fairbanks, Jr., 25 November 1940, PSF(C) 53: Great Britain, Kennedy.
[147] Dalton diary, 24 October 1940.
[148] Butler, *Lothian*, p. 290; cf. Lash, *Roosevelt and Churchill*, p. 196.
[149] PL to WSC, 29 August 1940, FO 800/398, US/40/22. In mid-June, amazed at the "staggering" change in American opinion over the previous few weeks, he thought it "would take very little to carry them in now—any kind of challenge by Hitler or Mussolini to their own vital interests would do it." (Letters of 12 June 1940, to Lady Astor in Astor papers, 4/49 and to Lady Minna Butler Thwing, LP 470: 13.) His change of view between then and August reflects partly his own ups and downs but, more significantly, the change in US mood once the French had collapsed and the dramatic fighting in Western Europe had come to an end.

was the progress of American rearmament to a point where the United States had an effective weapon in her hands. This, he judged, would not be before 1942.[150]

Lothian, therefore, did not see 5 November as a magic date. He believed that eventually the United States would provide the necessary assistance, but recognized that Britain could not sit back and wait. The end of the election was important because it enabled Britain to renew its pressure on the Administration and the American public. His thinking had been clearly stated in a cable on 21 September, in which he told the Foreign Office he wished to come home:

to discuss with you the formidable question we shall probably have to submit to United States Government immediately after Presidential election, and to obtain other information to enable me to present British case in speeches I shall have to make this Autumn and Winter. Public opinion here has not yet grasped that it will have to make far reaching decisions to finance and supply us and possibly still graver ones next Spring or Summer unless it is to take the responsibility of forcing us to make a compromised peace. Yet owing to size of country and its constitution it is usually impossible to get important decisions taken without at least six months preparation.[151]

After the election Britain waited expectantly for the United States to act. It waited in vain. Nothing was said or done about the dollar crisis, let alone about entering the war. Administration leaders went off for much-needed vacations and Washington lapsed into apparent lethargy. By the beginning of December British leaders were worried and uncertain. As Churchill told the Cabinet, he had been "rather chilled" by the United States attitude since the election.[152] It was Lothian who filled this vacuum in British policy. With no expectations of automatic results after 5 November, he was ready with two parallel foreign policy initiatives. One was to persuade Churchill to put Britain's whole position—strategic, economic, logistic—to the president. This took the form of the celebrated long letter of 8 December 1940 which Churchill later called "one of the most important I ever wrote."[153] The other *démarche* was to provoke public discussion and force the administration's hand by making calculated reference to Britain's problems at a press conference on his return to the United States on 23 November. These two initiatives deserve close attention. They represent the culmination of Lothian's diplomatic career and were significant contributions to the origins of Lend-Lease.

In his memoirs Churchill paid generous tribute to Lothian's achievements as ambassador. He also noted that it was Lothian "who urged me to write a full statement of our position to the President."[154] What is not

---

[150] PL to Hoare, 19 October 1940, Templewood papers, XIII/17 (Cambridge University Library).

[151] PL to FO, tel. 2063, 21 September 1940, A4534.

[152] CAB 65/10, WM 299 (40) 4, 2 December 1940.

[153] Churchill, *Second World War*, 2: 501.

[154] Ibid., p. 493.

clear from Churchill's account is that he was initially very reluctant to send the letter, and that even when convinced on that score he differed considerably with Lothian as to its contents. Lady Astor, Lothian's close friend, told her brother-in-law in January 1941 that

Philip . . . had a very difficult time making the P.M. see what he wanted to do in America. He felt that it was imperative that a strong note should go to the President telling him of our dire situation, particularly financially. It took him two weekends, one at Chequers and one at Dytchley but he finally got it done. Edward Halifax was a help.[155]

Lady Astor's report is substantiated by the official correspondence and drafts related to the 8 December letter.[156] The letter's history was as follows. As Churchill noted in his memoirs, it originated when Lothian was spending the weekend of 9–11 November with him at Dytchley Park.[157] Probably Lothian drew up a draft, which each subsequently revised. Meanwhile parts of the original draft went out for comment to responsible departments—principally the Treasury, the Admiralty and the Foreign Office. Each made suggestions, the Treasury in particular feeling that the sections on finance were not satisfactory.[158] On 18 November Churchill did some redrafting in the light of these comments. By then, however, Lothian had left for Washington. Despite his repeated urgings that the letter be sent as soon as possible there was a hiatus for more than a week. It was only on 27 November, after repeated pressure from the Foreign Office, that Churchill set matters in motion again. He asked Arthur Purvis, the head of British purchasing in the United States, who was then in London, to prepare a preliminary redraft. On 29 November Churchill dictated the whole letter at Chequers, after which the process of departmental consultation began anew. By now Roosevelt was about to embark on a post-election Caribbean cruise, and Churchill accepted Lothian's suggestion that the letter would have greater effect if delivered while the president was relaxing and reflecting rather than in the last-minute bustle before he left Washington. The Cabinet approved the text on 2 December, but three days later Lothian's very considerable revisions arrived. Most of these Churchill rejected. The letter was cabled to the Washington Embassy and Lothian sent the text to the State Department on the morning of 8 December. It is usually said that Roosevelt received it on the afternoon of the ninth, but, in fact, it may not have arrived until the morning of the eleventh.[159]

---

[155] Lady Astor to R. H. Brand, 17 January 1941, Astor papers, 3/14.
[156] This paragraph is based on PREM 3/486/1.
[157] For background to the weekend see Ronald Tree, *When the Moon Was High: Memoirs of Peace and War, 1897-1942*, pp. 130–133, 193.
[158] Cf. T 160/995, F19422, pp. 32–60.
[159] Robert E. Sherwood, *Roosevelt and Hopkins: An Intimate History*, p. 223 says that the letter arrived on the morning of 9 December with one of the prearranged deliveries by Navy seaplane of mail from Washington. On Lothian's covering letter to Hull of 8 December there are the annotations: "Forwarded to Navy 2:30 PM. Plane departed between 4 and 5 P.M. due in President's hands afternoon of 9th." (Hull papers, 48/141.) Cf. Warren F. Kimball,

Lothian's conception of this letter is quite clear. As he told Churchill on 12 November, "there was an opinion in Washington that we were inclined to ask for more than was necessary. The only answer to this is a ruthless exposé of the strategic dangers." The Foreign Office agreed. The previous day Cadogan noted in his diary that Lothian "had produced a very good message from P.M. for President putting all our cards on the table (which I think is right)."[160] This, of course, had been Lothian's tactic for some time. We saw, in connection with the Destroyers Deal, how he had given the pro-Allied pressure groups detailed and comprehensive information. In fact he had suggested that the government make a similar approach at that time to Roosevelt himself. Concerned at the latter's apparent pessimism after the Fall of France, Lothian had asked Churchill on 27 June for a "reasoned confidential statement showing not only our determination to fight to the finish, but giving grounds for hope and confidence," which Lothian could use to persuade the president to help Britain. Churchill had ignored the suggestion, emphasizing, probably correctly, that United States policy would be determined only by the result of the Battle of Britain and that the president "is our best friend."[161] It is probable that this confidence in the force of events and in Roosevelt's leadership—combined with his expectations about the election and his habitual preference for secrecy—account for Churchill's reluctance to send the letter in late November.

Further evidence of a basic difference of approach can be found in the circumstances under which Churchill was persuaded to take the matter up again at the end of the month. On 26 November Lothian cabled an account of his meeting with Roosevelt the previous day—the first since he had left America in mid-October. As warned, he said, he had found the president in a fatigued and depressed state of mind, unresponsive to any new ideas for action. This seemed to him typical of the general inertia in Washington. "After talking to the President and a number of people here," Lothian told the Foreign Office, "I am more convinced than ever of the importance of the Prime Minister's memorandum." The Foreign Office fully concurred.[162] It found other evidence to support Lothian. For some time the Foreign Office and the Admiralty had been badgering the United States Navy to release more destroyers. On 22 November the

---

The Most Unsordid Act: Lend-Lease 1939–1941, pp. 111–112. However, the log and records of the president's cruise show only two mail deliveries in this period: one leaving Washington on 7 December which reached FDR off Antigua on the morning of the ninth, the other on the tenth which reached him off the West Caicos Islands on the morning of the eleventh. There is no record of any special delivery. Furthermore, the list of contents of the mail pouch on 10 December includes an envelope from the British Embassy via the State Department, which would fit the circumstances of the 8 December letter. (See OF 200-1-F, Box 103—list and schedules, and Box 122, Log, pp. 14, 16–17).

[160] PL to WSC, 12 November 1940, PREM 3/486/1, p. 299. Cadogan, *Diaries*, 11 November 1940, p. 335.

[161] PL to WSC, tel. 1135, 27 June and WSC to PL, tel. 1304, 28 June 1940, PREM 3/476/10, pp. 531, 528.

[162] PL to FO, tel. 2802, 26 November, and Whitehead, minute, 27 November 1940, FO 371/24243, A4909/131/45.

British Embassy reported that "Knox had replied that this must be ruled out of the realm of what was possible." Scott minuted:

This kind of thing shows how important it is that the President should be given the full picture of our position and desiderata as set out in the draft message from the Prime Minister to Mr. Roosevelt drafted by Lord Lothian. I understand from No. 10 that the P.M. is still mulling it over. The sooner he can get something off the better.

Cadogan and Halifax agreed, the latter putting Scott's argument personally to Churchill. On the twenty-seventh the premier promised to get the letter ready in the next day or two.[163] This same philosophy was also urged by Arthur Purvis,. who wrote the preliminary redraft. Purvis suggested that Churchill should add a "confidential balance sheet" to dramatize Britain's needs by setting out on one side the forces and equipment probably needed to win the war and on the other those available in the Empire or currently expected from the United States. The difference between "credit" and "debit" columns would represent Britain's outstanding needs from the United States. Purvis explained:

In the past we have suffered by having fed our requirements to the United States "piece-meal." If the suggestion now made be adopted, the President would be personally presented with a comprehensive picture, a course which I understood from my last conversation with him and with Secretary Morgenthau he would welcome. It is only through placing such a picture in the President's hands that the U.S. Administration can be brought to visualize the necessary sacrifices in finance, suspension of labour regulations, restrictions on industry, etc.[164]

But even when Churchill had taken up the letter again, the disagreements were not over. After dictating his revised version on the twenty-ninth, the Prime Minister cabled Lothian: "I am reluctant to make any additions as I wish to focus on shipping."[165] That did not deter the ambassador, who cabled his own amendments on the night of 4–5 December. He had rewritten most of the last quarter of the letter, partly to bring out the financial problem more fully, he said, but above all "to keep the perspective right without deducting from the shipping case."[166] The general feeling was that Lothian's version was too detailed. Specific information could be sent later, perhaps to the appropriate United States department heads rather than to the president. According to Halifax, the premier "did not like much of Lothian's stuff which he thought verbose and suffering from an over-attempt at being comprehensive!" Halifax agreed. He argued that Churchill alone could give the letter its final shape, as the product of his own mind rather than a composite effort, and that

---

[163] Ibid., A4790, esp. Butler to FO, tel. 2754A, 22 November; minute by Scott, 25 November; Halifax to Vansittart, 28 November and to WSC, 28 November 1940.

[164] Purvis, memo, 28 November, PREM 3/486/1, p. 244.

[165] WSC to PL, tel. 3290, 30 November 1940, A4790. In his draft of this message Churchill had continued ". . . and not start too many hares running all over the world at once." (PREM 3/486/1, p. 218.)

[166] PL to WSC, tel., 5 December 1940, PREM 3/486/1, p. 190.

this consideration must take priority if necessary over logical completeness or particular points of emphasis. Halifax was surely correct. But Lothian's approach was explained and supported in a fascinating minute from Scott on 6 December:

The Prime Minister was, I believe, mainly concerned to concentrate on the shipping, but Lord Lothian obviously still thinks that it would be better to give the President a full picture *now*, and I think he is right. His idea was that this letter should be continuously in the President's mind and that its existence and the knowledge that some day it might be published would act as a continual spur in meeting our requirements for fear lest it should be said in years to come "he knew, he was warned and he didn't take the necessary steps."[167]

Even a cursory reading of the 8 December letter confirms that Churchill's primary emphasis *was* on the shipping problem. The text ran to over 4,000 words. More than half was devoted to shipping, in addition to a detailed statistical appendix setting out the shipping losses for 1940. Finance, by contrast, took up about 400 words at the end. Churchill's language reinforced his allocation of space. It was "in shipping and in the power to transport across the oceans, particularly the Atlantic Ocean," he told the president, "that in 1941 the crunch of the whole war will be found."[168] On finance, Churchill warned that: "The moment approaches when we shall no longer be able to pay cash for shipping and other supplies." But his main point in that section was that Britain should not be forced to sell off all her assets before the United States provided financial help.

Despite this imbalance, however, the letter still provided the synoptic view of Britain's situation for which Lothian had been striving. It set Britain's cards on the table with striking candor and completeness. After stating London's assumptions about the "solid identity of interest" between the two countries, Churchill summarized the developments of 1940 and set out the prospects for 1941. He discussed the three great interrelated problems of shipping, munitions, and finance, drawing out Britain's requirements from the United States in each case. Without American escorts, extended patrolling, and the use "of every ton of merchant shipping" that she possessed, the Royal Navy could not keep open the supply routes to Britain and to her battlefronts around the world. Without United States munitions, especially aircraft, Britain could not arm herself or her allies. Without financial aid, Britain would not be able to acquire the shipping and munitions she needed. This, Churchill concluded, was "a statement of the minimum action necessary to the achievement of our common purpose."

---

[167] Ibid., pp. 181–183; minutes by Halifax, 7 December, and Scott, 6 December, A4790.

[168] The FO printed text has "crux" for "crunch"—the import is much the same. The text is printed in e.g., Woodward, *British Foreign Policy* 1: 388–395; Churchill, *Second World War* 2: 494–501; *FRUS*, 1940, 3: 18–26. FDR's copy is in MR 1/1.

In a telegram on 13 December 1940, Churchill made the same point. "North Atlantic transport remains the prime anxiety," he told the president. (See PREM 3/468, pp. 13–15.)

In summary, then, Lothian persuaded Churchill to send Roosevelt an overview of Britain's position and needs. Churchill was initially reluctant but came round to the idea by the end of November. However, he wanted to treat shipping as the fundamental issue, at the expense of comprehensiveness or balance,, and the financial question was discussed briefly and without the same sense of urgency. Yet in his memoirs Churchill placed this letter firmly within the context of Britain's dollar crisis and the origins of Lend-Lease. Historians have followed his example, and they have been right to do so. But the fact that this letter became a central part of the Lend-Lease story was due less to its own content and origins as to the climate of opinion Lothian had already helped to create in the United States before its arrival. This leads us to the second line of diplomacy adopted by Lothian after the election—his celebrated remarks when he arrived in New York on the morning of 23 November 1940.

There has been some misunderstanding as to what Lothian said on this occasion. Most historians have followed Sir John Wheeler-Bennett in stating that Lothian simply told the waiting press: "Well, boys, Britain's broke, its your money we want." But it is clear from press reports and from Lothian's account sent to the Foreign Office that he said far more than this. Indeed it is questionable that he ever used those notorious words.[169] On arrival at La Guardia Lothian made this brief statement:

The first half of 1940 was Hitler's year. The second half, we think, is ours. He failed in his plans to smash our fleet and perhaps invade England.

There is no doubt of its being a hard war. Two hundred lives are lost daily in the bombing raids and 300 people are injured.

Next year, too, we know will be long and hard. England will be grateful for any help. England needs planes, munitions, ships and perhaps a little financial help.[170]

Later he expanded on this statement and answered reporters' questions in an office in the airport building. Among other things he stressed Britain's

---

[169] Most historians quote from the initial reference, in Sir John's excellent official biography of King George VI: "'Well, boys, Britain's broke, it's your money we want.' Such was the realistic message offered by Lord Lothian to the crowd of pressmen who had assembled to meet him at La Guardia Airport on his last return from England in November 1940; and his words set off a chain of events in America which culminated some four months later in the enactment of the Lend-Lease legislation." (John W. Wheeler-Bennett, *King George VI: His Life and Reign*, p. 521.) In his memoirs Sir John amplified this aside, saying that he and Aubrey Morgan of the British Press Service in New York met Lothian at La Guardia, that they told him the press was clamoring for a statement and that, after a moment's thought, Lothian simply and deliberately uttered the famous words and passed through to the waiting car. (Sir John Wheeler-Bennett, *Special Relationships: America in Peace and War*, p. 112.) In addition to the sources cited below, I have drawn upon *New York Herald Tribune*, 24 November 1940, pp. 1, 19; and Aubrey N. Morgan, letter to author, 11 July 1979, and conversation of 11 November 1979. Morgan believes that although Lothian probably used the phrase "Britain is bust" in his press conference he made no mention of needing United States money. His own recollection is that Sir John was not present at La Guardia, and that is also my own conclusion. It would seem that Sir John's account of the episode derived from subsequent conversation with Morgan and that, by the time he came to write his memoirs, the story had become considerably distorted in his memory.
[170] *New York Times*, 24 November 1940, 7: 4.

confidence in ultimate victory, said that she definitely did not need men, and refused to be drawn on the question of how the United States should respond to Britain's plight, asserting that this was for Americans to decide. On finance, press reports quote him as saying that the matter was "becoming urgent," and that "available gold and securities had been virtually used up and that this factor figured in the calculations for 1941." Lothian told the Foreign Office: "I mentioned no figures of any kind but indicated that the question of how to pay for munitions would be one of the problems which would come up certainly in the next 6 months, as our resources including gold and securities were running low."[171]

There is no evidence that Lothian acted with the permission of his government. The furor his remarks provoked in London testifies to this, and Lothian himself admitted to Morgenthau on 2 December that he had spoken on his own authority.[172] But, as historians have inferred, this was clearly a premeditated act. The head of the Foreign Office's American Department minuted on 28 November:

Lord Lothian pointed out to us during his visit that it takes the American public, on whom the Executive depend for getting their policies approved, at least six months to demand action on an idea from the time it is mooted. I am convinced that he had this consideration in mind when he made the remarks. . . .

And Sir Walter Layton, the newspaper owner and a senior official in the Ministry of Supply, who talked with Lothian in early December, later wrote:

That statement was deliberate. He knew it would create excitement but during his stay at Lisbon [where Lothian had to wait a week for the plane to New York] he made up his mind that the American public must get used to the idea that Great Britain needed financial help. He meant to bring the matter to a head for he felt it would not be honest to go on pretending that we could pay.[173]

However, it is also clear that Lothian was not making an emotive appeal for immediate credits. His formal statement was effectively a summary of the impending letter to Roosevelt, setting out all Britain's main needs in 1941. In his remarks afterwards Lothian seems to have concentrated on finance. This was partly because he considered that to be the most critical question and partly because he probably wanted to prepare the American

---

[171] *New York Times*, 24 November, 1: 5; *Sunday Dispatch* (London), 24 November 1940, 1: 4; PL to FO, tel. 2793, 24 November 1940, FO 371/24249, A4935/434/45. Lothian later reiterated the main points of his remarks at La Guardia for Washington correspondents when he arrived at Union Station—see *Washington Post*, 24 November 1940, 1: 4–5 and 5: 4.

[172] MD 342A: 1.

[173] Balfour, minute, 28 November 1940, FO 371/24243, A4891/131/45; enclosure to Layton to Lord Samuel, 10 February 1941, in Samuel papers, A114/6a (HLRO). Layton told Churchill: "Throughout his last fortnight, Philip remained confident, in spite of some public and private criticism in America, that he had made no mistake in broaching the financial question on his arrival in New York. He was certain that the President would come over handsomely when the situation was put before him, but he felt that some preparation of public opinion was necessary if quick action was to be taken. He was quite satisfied with the reaction of public opinion." (Layton to WSC, 3 January 1941, PREM 4/25/8, pp. 488–90.).

public for the visit of Sir Frederick Phillips from the British Treasury in early December.[174] But even in those informal remarks he did not make an appeal for immediate help. It seems that he wanted to start a debate about Britain's general position, particularly financial, so that the necessary measures would be taken in time, given the slowness of the United States political process.

The problem was that, once again, Lothian had not been sufficiently careful in handling a delicate issue. He failed to make it quite clear that in talking of Britain's financial problems he was referring only to her ability to purchase from the United States, and not her overall financial position. Probably he did make this point during his informal remarks, but not with the reiterated emphasis necessary before letting such an arcane and complex topic fall into the hands of journalists and headline-writers. The Associated Press report, which most papers outside New York used as the basis of their stories, stated, without qualification, that Lothian had said that Britain "was beginning to come to the end of her financial resources." The Reuters account, widely circulated abroad, used the same phrase.[175] Anglophobe and isolationist papers seized on the comment. "Envoy Lothian claims Britain is going broke," was the *Chicago Tribune's* headline. German propaganda had a field day, and from Sweden to West Africa the Foreign Office received reports of the demoralizing effect the news of Britain's supposedly impending bankruptcy was having on world opinion.[176] The British Treasury was furious. Lothian's initiative seemed reckless and unnecessary in view of Phillips' imminent visit. They were only prevented from sending an indignant telegram when Churchill agreed to chastize Lothian himself. "We are so closely united in thought and friendship," the Prime Minister began, "that I feel you will not mind my making a few comments on your recent remarks." In part his gentle but firm rebuke was directed at the careless language and the failure to consult the Treasury. But Churchill also questioned Lothian's whole approach. "I do not think it was wise to touch on very serious matters to reporters on the landing stage. It is safer to utter a few heartening generalities and leave the graver matters to be raised formally with the President or his chief lieutenants."[177] Here, again, was the difference of tactics between the two men—the argument as to the rival merits of waiting for Roosevelt or going public to help mobilize the support and pressure the president needed before he could act.

Although wishing to start a debate, Lothian probably did not intend to spark off such a furious controversy. He was at pains, subsequently,

---

[174] Cf. PL to Morgenthau, 25 November 1940, MD 332: 266 and also MD 331: 295.

[175] E.g. *San Francisco Chronicle*, 24 November 1940, p. 1 (AP); *Sunday Dispatch*, 24 November 1: 4 (Reuters).

[176] *Chicago Tribune*, 24 November 1940, p. 1; Press attaché, Stockholm, to MOI, Empax tel. 242, 28 November 1940, FO 371/24243, p. 278; Robertson to Waley, 28 November and Maling to Robertson, 27 November, T160/1089, F16041/8, and Hodson to Robertson, 30 November 1940, T160/1051, F17286/01.

[177] T160/995, F19422, pp. 64–65; Scott, minute, 24 November 1940 and WSC to PL, tel. 3233, 27 November, FO 371/24249, A4935/434/45.

to play down somewhat the significance of his remarks. After seeing Roosevelt on 25 November, for instance, he immediately spoke to waiting pressmen: " 'The President and I never mentioned finances,' said the Ambassador. He rushed over to newspaper correspondents to make this statement even before he took his hat down from the rack in the White House waiting room."[178] In view of his government's disapproval, Lothian also deemed it politic to eat humble pie. "I am extremely sorry that I should have raised the question of dollar finance without obtaining the prior approval of the Chancellor of the Exchequer," he cabled on 28 November. "I should like to apologize to him. I will see this mistake is not repeated." But he went on to defend his conduct with a vigor that showed he was basically unrepentant:

In this as in every other question the ultimate determinant is public opinion. That opinion is saturated with illusions to the effect that we have vast resources available which have not been disclosed, that it is possible for us to mobilise all the American assets and all the assets of our Dominions and our allies as well as our properties in the Empire and in foreign countries and make them available in dollars for paying for munitions and that we ought to empty this vast hypothetical barrel before we ask for assistance.

He added that even the president entertained dangerous illusions about Britain's ability to go on paying for American purchases. He was convinced that the heated discussion he had provoked would gradually convince Americans of the urgency of the situation. He also emphasized that this was only one facet of the fundamental question now before the United States of whether to help Britain within the limits of neutrality or to keep her going even at risk of eventual United States entry into the war. Debate on that question, he concluded, would be greatly stimulated by Churchill's letter to Roosevelt.[179]

Was Lothian correct? The Foreign Office thought that he was and that the long-term effect of his remarks on United States opinion would be beneficial.[180] Support for this judgment came from the British Press Service in New York, who for more than a year had been monitoring the major United States papers and radio commentators with growing shrewdness and skill. In a full-scale report on media reaction to the interview, dated 4 December, the British Press Service stated that for over a week Lothian's comments had inspired an exceptionally large volume of comment in papers of every size all over the country. Lothian had focused discussion of Anglo-American cooperation on the question of finance. Other topics, such as naval and shipping aid, had been temporarily overshadowed. Despite his lack of qualifications, the British Press Service judged that editors and commentators understood and had made clear that Lothian

---

[178] *New York Times*, 26 November 1940, 4: 1–2.

[179] PL to Halifax for WSC, tel. 2843, 28 November 1940, T160/995, F19422, p. 91. For Lothian's lack of contrition, see recollections in Richard G. Casey, *Personal Experience, 1939–1946*, p. 43 and Wheeler-Bennett, *Special Relationships*, pp. 112–113.

[180] Minutes of 25–28 November 1940, FO 371/24243, p. 270.

was talking only of Britain's dollar problem. It concluded that: "The interview precipitated realistic discussion of the purpose and implications of the whole so-called 'Aid-to-Britain' policy, a question hitherto generally discussed in a vague if well-meaning manner."[181] That was surely what Lothian had intended. It was the pebble-in-the-pool technique that we identified earlier. His remarks brought Britain's financial problem from the obscure parts of newspapers on to the front page. His visits to see United States leaders and the intense debate among editors and columnists kept it in the public eye until Phillips' arrival on 4 December. Phillips's discussions gave it renewed momentum until Roosevelt's famous press conference on 17 December, when he announced the principle of Lend-Lease. One need not postulate that most Americans took any notice. What counted was that Lothian clearly brought the issue to the attention of the opinion leaders and key policy-making groups whose support would be essential for the enactment of any legislation.

Had Lothian not acted, no one else in British officialdom would have done so. In theory, one might consider Sir Frederick Phillips a possible candidate. Phillips, after all, had come to discuss the dollar problem, and he had admitted privately in November that the "main difficulty is that our financial weakness has been so successfully concealed that outside Administration circles no one in the United States has the least notion of its gravity. Even President Roosevelt seems to think that the crisis is some six months off."[182] But Phillips, though very shrewd, was a taciturn and colorless official, with little flair for publicity. Like most British civil servants he found the direct, informal, and open character of press–government relations in the United States unsettling and distasteful. In January he wrote home about what he termed "the government of a country by the Press. It is literally true that nothing happens which is not in the papers within a day or two." The concept of confidentiality was quite foreign to Americans, Phillips felt. "So you either do no business at all or do it through the newspapers."[183] Clearly Phillips was not the man to "educate" the American public. The most obvious department of British government for this tak was, of course, the Ministry of Information. Even before Lothian's press conference its American division, staffed by academics and journalists who knew and understood the United States, was pressing for a post-election publicity campaign to explain Britain's predicament to America. This pressure intensified after Lothian's statement. But the Ministry of Information was a temporary wartime ministry, firmly under the thumb of the permanent Whitehall departments. The Foreign Office, Treasury, and Churchill felt that this was a delicate moment and

---

[181] BPS 79, 4 December 1940, FO 371/24244, A4995/131/45. See also files of *New York Times, Washington Post, Chicago Tribune* and *San Francisco Chronicle* for November and December 1940.

[182] Phillips, minute, 12 November 1940, T160/995, F19422, p. 47. For a similar comment by Keynes see p. 49.

[183] Phillips to Sir Richard Hopkins, 14 January 1941, T175/121.

that Britain should wait upon the Administration rather than risk reviving the American propaganda phobia. The Ministry of Information was kept on a tight rein throughout the period of Lend-Lease.[184]

If Lothian helped stimulate public debate about Britain's situation, did his remarks have any direct effect on the Administration? Joseph Lash thinks not, emphasizing that a month before the arrival of Churchill's letter and two weeks before Lothian returned to New York "American leaders were thinking of how to relieve Britain's dollar problem."[185] As Lash points out, Roosevelt observed on 8 November:

that the time would surely come when Great Britain would need loans or credits. He suggested that one way to meet the situation would be for us to supply whatever we could under leasing arrangements with England. For instance, he thought that we could lease ships or any other property that was loanable, returnable, and insurable.[186]

This record by Ickes shows clearly that the concept of Lend-Lease was in the president's mind before Lothian spoke out. Indeed, one might trace the concept right back to November 1938.[187] But it is also clear that at this stage Roosevelt did not think Britain's dollar situation was urgent or that his leasing idea had more than specific application. On 8 November, according to Ickes, Roosevelt had prefaced his remarks by saying "that England still has sufficient credits and property in this country to finance additional war supplies. He thinks that the British have about $2.5 billion here in credit and property that could be liquidated. He believes that this money ought to be spent first, although the British do not want to liquidate their American securities." And the day before Roosevelt had talked in a similar vein to Arthur Purvis. He raised the question of Britain's dollar resources, but it was clear, Purvis felt, that he thought the problem was still six months away. The president's principal anxiety was Britain's merchant shipping position. He felt that the United States should build 300 ships and then "rent them" to Britain, who would also pay for the insurance. "He indicated that this system might be extended to cover certain other similar items."[188]

Lothian's comments did not have an immediate effect on the president's thinking. On 1 December, just before leaving on his Caribbean cruise, Roosevelt talked over the situation with Morgenthau.[189] He still did not

---

[184] See papers in INF 1/872.

[185] Lash, *Roosevelt and Churchill*, p. 260.

[186] Ickes, *Secret Diary* 3: 367.

[187] At a White House meeting on 14 November 1938 FDR outlined his policy on rearmament and support for Britain and France. He said: "Had we had this summer 5,000 planes and the capacity immediately to produce 10,000 per year, even though I might have had to ask Congress for authority to sell or lend them to the countries in Europe, Hitler would not have dared to take the stand he did." (MD 150: 338.) For a possible World War I precedent see Kimball, *Most Unsordid Act*, p. 123.

[188] Ickes, *Secret Diary*, 3: 367; Purvis to Salter, tel. Pursa 218, 10 November 1940, FO 371/25149, W11700/79/49. (FDR aired the leasing idea again on 28 November, in conversation with Lamont and Norman Davis. See Lamont papers, 127–25.)

[189] MD 334: 1–4.

believe that Britain's immediate financial position was critical. After a cursory glance at a United States Treasury estimate of Britain's dollar resources he threw it on the desk and said "Well, they aren't bust—there's lots of money there." What worried Roosevelt was that the British could no longer provide the capital investment to accelerate United States rearmament. He believed that America should now make a large investment in plant and new orders, and the British could pay for their share of the output. He still saw his loan idea as applicable mainly to merchant shipping. Roosevelt also believed that this program did not require congressional approval. The capital investment and new orders for munitions and ships could be financed from Reconstruction Finance Corporation funds. However, he clearly was reluctant to state all this explicitly in writing, and give his Cabinet the authorization they wanted. In discussions after he had left, there was a general feeling among responsible officials, particularly Stimson and the RFC head, Jesse Jones, that they had reached the acceptable limits of executive action and that the Administration must go to Congress for clear authority.[190]

When Roosevelt left Washington on 2 December for his cruise, therefore, he still believed that Britain's problems could be met by an extension of existing executive policies with the addition of some kind of loan arrangement with regard to merchant shipping. By the time he returned two weeks later he had pulled together his ideas into a comprehensive program for all Britain's supply needs, based on the loan idea and backed by congressional approval.[191] The reasons for this development are not clear but can be inferred. Undoubtedly the cruise provided an opportunity for relaxation and reflection. Not only Lothian but also close associates of the president such as Welles and Bullitt testified that he had been unusually tired and depressed after the election and right through November. The vacation gave him time to draw together various half-formed ideas and, as on other such occasions, proved the prelude to a major policy initiative.[192] It is also likely, as contemporaries and historians have argued, that Churchill's letter had a considerable effect.[193] In view of what has just been said, however, about the contents and origins of the letter, its effect was probably due less to its comments on finance than to its synoptic character and the way it brought out the interrelationship of Britain's problems. In other words it did not arouse Roosevelt to the dollar problem so much as make clear to him the need for a comprehensive solution to Britain's needs.

The importance of Lothian's comments lay in the fact that they forced Roosevelt to act quickly. This, it should be stressed, was not because the

---

[190] Cf. Kimball, *Most Unsordid Act*, pp. 108, 113–114.

[191] MPD 3: 740, 17 December 1940.

[192] Moffat, diary, vol. 46, "Washington visit, 24–27 November 1940," p. 12 (Welles); Ickes, *Secret Diary* 3: 374, entry for 23 November (Bullitt); cf. Casey, *Personal Experience*, p. 18, PL, tel. 2802, 26 November, cited in note 162, and Sherwood, *Roosevelt and Hopkins*, p. 224.

[193] See Kimball, *Most Unsordid Act*, pp. 119–120.

president changed his mind about Britain's financial position. He informed the press on his return that the British had plenty of exchange to pay for existing orders, and the following March he told a surprised Morgenthau "that he always had in mind that they would have enough money to last until the first of May."[194] This belief helps to explain his pressure on the British during early 1941 to sell off securities and investments in the United States. What Lothian had done was to generate public debate and anxiety which forced the Administration to clarify its position. That anxiety had some unfortunate effects for Britain. For one thing, as Allied officials later remarked privately, its immediate result was "to frighten hell out of the contractors" with whom Britain was about to place orders.[195] It also placed the Administration in a difficult position with Congress. As Morgenthau pointed out to Lothian on 2 December, some isolationist senator could now call him up to the Hill and say "Well, on such and such a date Ambassador Lothian said the English were running short of money. By what authority did you let them place additional orders in this country?" This, Morgenthau noted, "seemed a new idea" to Lothian.[196] It is clear, in fact, that Lothian's remarks, as distorted in the press, were one reason for the difficulties Britain experienced during the period of "interim finance" between late November 1940 and the passage of the Lend-Lease legislation the following March. But Morgenthau also admitted on 2 December that Lothian's statement "had forced the President and himself to deal with the cash problem immediately." Although convinced that Britain could still finance immediate needs, they had to clarify the Administration's long-term policy on the question to head off congressional criticism. As Lothian told the Foreign Office: "The effect of recent events is that the President and the Secretary will have to explain our dollar position to Congress in the near future and obtain authority from it as to how it should be dealt with."[197]

What, then, was Lothian's contribution to the origins of Lend-Lease? Unlike most British leaders he did not believe that Roosevelt's reelection would lead quickly and automatically to an extension of United States assistance to Britain. He was therefore ready with two initiatives to stimulate public debate and influence the Administration. He persuaded a reluctant Churchill to send Roosevelt a candid appreciation of Britain's

---

[194] FDR, press conference 702, 17 December 1940, in *The Public Papers and Addresses of Franklin D. Roosevelt*, ed. Samuel I. Rosenman, 9: 610; MPD 4: 852, 10 March 1941. And PL told London on 28 November 1940, presumably after talking with Lamont: "the President said in private today to Thomas Lamont that he believed that we could go on paying to July 1942 and that it was therefore premature to raise the issue now." (Tel. cited in note 179.)

[196] MD 342A: 1, memo of conversation with PL on 2 December 1940.

[197] PL to FO, tel. 2911, 4 December 1940, FO 371/25209, W11960/8940/49. Cf. H. Duncan Hall, *North American Supply*, p. 258. The recently-opened evidence therefore confirms Warren Kimball's earlier judgment (*Most Unsordid Act*, p. 96) that Lothian's remarks "provided the catalyst that forced the Roosevelt Administration publicly to face up to the question of the British dollar shortage."

On interim finance see Warren F. Kimball, "'Beggar My Neighbor': America and the British Interim Finance Crisis, 1940–1941," pp. 758–772.

whole situation. He also explained that situation, and especially the dollar gap, publicly on his return to the United States. Roosevelt was beginning to face up to this problem, but Lothian's remarks, or rather the press reports of them, sparked off a major press and political debate which obliged him to act. Churchill's letter, arriving during a much-needed vacation when he had time to think, helped force the president into a comprehensive program for presentation to Congress. Lothian's remarks had some unfortunate side-effects, which he probably did not foresee. They unsettled world opinion, complicated Britain's interim finance, and led the Administration to concentrate on the Lend-Lease bill in the next few months to the detriment of other pressing issues, such as industrial mobilization and the shipping crisis. But Lothian was probably right that the Administration had to be forced into a new policy. With Britain nearing the end of her financial and shipping resources, the limits of Roosevelt's policy of "cash and carry" neutrality had been reached. To be effective a new policy required congressional approval and support. And, as Lothian anticipated, it took about six months to translate that policy from idea into reality.

VII. Conclusion: Verdict
on an Ambassadorship

L othian did not live to see the results of his labors. He died suddenly on 12 December 1940 from uremic poisoning, having refused medical treatment in accordance with his Christian Science beliefs. Ironically, he was succeeded by Halifax, the man who had pushed through Lothian's own appointment, and whom Churchill now wanted to get rid of. Eventually Halifax proved a capable and effective ambassador, but his first year was not impressive. Arthur Purvis, whose own role in Anglo-American relations in this period still awaits full scholarly recognition, was one of many to compare him unfavorably with his predecessor. In June 1941 "Purvis missed Lord Lothian whom he considered a great vitalizer. He admitted he made many mistakes, but on balance rated him as a very great British representative. Lord Halifax he found unimaginative and terse, less interested in formulating policy than in carrying out instructions."[198]

As Purvis observed, assessing Lothian's achievement is very much a question of balance. In some respects the Foreign Office had been right at the time of his appointment to question his discretion and judgment. As his old friend and mentor Lloyd George put it in November 1940: "He is usually so concentrating upon one particular aspect of a situation that it excludes any concentrated attention upon other aspects."[199] Lothian's Yale speech of 19 June 1940 and the side-effects of his 23 November press conference are examples of this. In such periods of heightened anxiety Lothian also tended to neglect the details of a problem in his pursuit of an overriding goal, as we saw when discussing his 18 July proposal for an oil embargo and his handling of the destroyers negotiations in August. There is therefore some truth in Hugh Dalton's caustic criticisms that Lothian was "very fond of 'large ideas', particularly in a vague and unfinished form" and that "his strong suit is high-minded ballyhoo. This may be quite useful in America so long as the policy of H.M.G. has not to be too exactly based upon it."[200] Dalton was also right that at times Lothian's desire for Anglo-American cooperation impaired his effectiveness as an advocate of British policy. This seems to have been the case in the autumn of 1940 over oil and the blockade.

---

[198] Moffat, diary, 17 June 1941.
[199] Lloyd George to Liddell Hart, 19 November 1940, Lloyd George papers, G/9/3/44 (HLRO).
[200] Dalton diary, 24 October, 9 November 1940.

Yet this is only one side of the account. Oliver Harvey, who, in 1939, had been one of the keenest Foreign Office critics of Lothian's selection, wrote after his death: "In spite of all our misgivings L. proved himself a very great Ambassador and he will be very hard indeed to replace."[201] At risk of simplification one can identify three main reasons for Lothian's success. In each case his approach to Anglo-American relations offers an interesting contrast with that of Churchill.

First, he built up a close relationship of mutual trust with American leaders. In part this trust was based upon the similarity between his own liberal convictions and the thinking of Roosevelt and the New Dealers. Even an inveterate anglophobe such as Adolf Berle in the State Department quickly took a liking to Lothian.[202] In part it was the result of his policy of not assuming American help but providing information to justify British requests and acting in an open and cooperative manner to dispel American suspicions. Churchill was slow to adopt this tactic. In the summer he delayed British offers of bases and military secrets, hoping to tie them to an acceptable American quid pro quo, and in November he was reluctant to put all Britain's cards on the table in a message to the president.

Second, Lothian understood that effective pressure on the Administration depended on mobilizing public support. He quickly built up an easy and open relationship with the press. He spoke out in speeches and press conferences to explain Britain's needs in terms calculated to win American support. He leaked sensitive information, notably in late July and on 23 November, to help opinion leaders stimulate debate and apply pressure on the Administration. This was not Churchill's way. He feared that publicizing Britain's secrets could aid the enemy and disturb domestic morale. He also believed that Britain should not pay too much attention "to the eddies of United States opinion." Rather than public diplomacy Churchill preferred to wait on the "force of events" and on the response of "our best friend"—the president.[203]

Last, Lothian had a clear-cut and plausible argument for Anglo-American cooperation, which he reiterated with the persistence and simplicity of a good public-relations man. In July 1941, reading the published edition of Lothian's American speeches, Halifax felt "sure we owe him a great deal for getting so firmly into their heads how great a part the British fleet, resting on its world strategic bases, played throughout the nineteenth century in enabling the United States to make the Monroe Doctrine a reality."[204] As Walter Lippmann observed to J. M. Keynes in April 1942, Lothian's death left "almost a complete intellectual vacuum." No responsible British leader enunciated any clear philosophy of Anglo-American relations.[205] Halifax was not a publicist, while Churchill preferred the lan-

---

[201] Harvey, TS. diary, 14 December 1940 (British Library, London, Add. MSS. 56397).
[202] Cf. Berle, diary, 1 and 22 September 1939 (FDRL).
[203] Quotations from WSC to PL, tel. 1304, 28 June 1940, PREM 3/476/10, p. 528.
[204] Halifax, diary, 5 July 1941, A 7.8.8, p. 77.
[205] Lippmann to Keynes, 2 April 1942, Lippmann papers 82/1217 (Sterling Library, Yale University).

guage of kin and common culture, which might have been effective in the
stirring days of 1940 but sounded increasingly anachronistic as the war
progressed. Lothian had appealed to America's interests rather than to
sentiment. Not only did his speeches provide an intellectual foundation
for Anglo-American alliance, they also helped to popularize the "realist"
tradition of thinking about an Atlantic community which was increasingly
to dominate United States diplomacy after World War II.[206]

There is good reason therefore to concur in the judgment of Sir James
Butler, Lothian's biographer and also the historian of British wartime grand
strategy. Commenting on Lothian's death, he wrote:

Exactly a year was to pass before the United States entered the war, but she was
already "in effect a non-belligerent ally"; and perhaps no one except the President,
the Prime Minister—and Hitler, had contributed more to this result than the man
who, as Philip Kerr, had long shown an instinctive understanding of the American
outlook.[207]

Yet it is also probable that by the end of 1940 Lothian's most important
work had been accomplished. He had been ideally suited to a fluid and
uncertain period when the Anglo-American alliance was being created
and the ambassador had to be a jack-of-all-trades. By 1941 the texture
of the relationship had changed. The Roosevelt-Churchill axis was becoming the major channel of communication, top level emissaries were
bypassing the official ambassadors, and much of the complex detail was
handled by special missions. Undoubtedly Halifax was better qualified to
preside over the mini-Whitehall that proliferated along Massachusetts
Avenue, and, as Sir John Wheeler-Bennett observed, it is difficult to imagine Lothian reduced to the role of "messenger-boy" between the two great
national leaders.[208] Furthermore, by the time of Lothian's death Roosevelt
was coming round to the idea he had summarily rejected when Lothian
had pressed it upon him in January 1939. Under the pressure of unforeseen
and revolutionary events America *would* have to fill the vacuum created
by the contraction of British power.

This is not to say that Lothian could have contributed little to Anglo-
American understanding in 1941 and after. It *is* to say that Lothian, like
Churchill, probably reached the pinnacle of his public life in 1940. As
Churchill told the Commons on 19 December:

---

[206] This tradition awaits its historian, though there are suggestive discussions in Robert E.
Osgood, *Ideals and Self-Interest in America's Foreign Relations*, pp. 387–400 and Alan K.
Henrikson, "The Map as an 'Idea': The Role of Cartographic Imagery during the Second
World War," pp. 19–53. This relative neglect of "the intellectual history of American foreign
policy" seems to reflect the recent preoccupation of American diplomatic historians with
treating United States policy largely as the outcome of economic imperatives or bureaucratic
politics. Cf. J. A. Thompson, "From the Monroe Doctrine to the Marshall Plan," p. 745.

[207] J. R. M. Butler, *Grand Strategy*, 2: 421. His evaluation of Lothian's career is in Butler,
Lothian, pp. 314–321.

[208] Wheeler-Bennett, *Special Relationships*, p. 116. For hints of a similar view, see Butler,
Lothian, p. 319. Lothian had made it clear at the time of his appointment that he wished
to serve for only two or, at the most, three years. (PL to Halifax, 8 August 1938, FO
794/18.)

. . . I cannot help feeling that to die at the height of a man's career, the highest moment of his effort here in this world, universally honoured and admired, to die while great issues are still commanding the whole of his interest, to be taken from us at the moment when he could already see ultimate success in view—is not the most unenviable of fates."[209]

It was an eloquent, generous and, perhaps, wistful tribute.

---

[209] House of Commons, *Debates*, 5th series, vol. 367, cols. 1398–1399, 19 December 1940.

BIBLIOGRAPHY

Only materials cited in this monograph or directly used in its preparation are listed here. For a fuller bibliography see Reynolds, *The Creation of the Anglo-American Alliance.*

I. MANUSCRIPTS: GREAT BRITAIN

Birmingham, University Library
  Neville Chamberlain, papers and diaries (NC)
Cambridge, University Library
  Templewood papers
Edinburgh, Scottish Record Office (SRO)
  Philip Kerr, 11th Marquis of Lothian [GD 40/17] (LP)
London, British Library
  Lord Harvey of Tasburgh, diaries
London, British Library of Political and Economic Science
  Hugh Dalton, papers and diaries
London, House of Lords Record Office (HLRO)
  David Lloyd George, papers
  Herbert, Lord Samuel, papers
London, Public Record Office (PRO)
  Admiralty (ADM)
  Cabinet Office (CAB)
  Foreign Office (FO)
  Ministry of Information (INF)
  Prime Minister's Office (PREM)
  Treasury (T)
Oxford, Bodleian Library
  Lord Altrincham [Sir Edward Grigg], papers
Reading, University Library
  Nancy, Viscountess Astor, papers
York, Borthwick Institute
  Edward, 1st Earl of Halifax, diaries (Hickleton papers)

II. MANUSCRIPTS: UNITED STATES OF AMERICA

Boston, Harvard University Business School, Baker Library
  Thomas W. Lamont, papers
Cambridge, Mass., Harvard University, Houghton Library
  J. Pierrepont Moffat, diaries and papers
Chapel Hill, N.C., University of North Carolina, Southern Historical Collection
  Frank P. Graham, papers
Hyde Park, N.Y., Franklin D. Roosevelt Library (FDRL)
  Adolf A. Berle, diary
  Henry Morgenthau, Jr., papers, diaries (MD) and presidential diaries (MPD)
  Franklin D. Roosevelt (FDR)
    Map Room files (MR)
    Official files (OF)
    President's Personal files (PPF)
    President's Secretary's files (PSF)
  Whitney H. Shepardson, papers
New Haven, Ct., Yale University, Sterling Library
  Walter Lippmann, papers
  Henry L. Stimson, diary

61

Washington, D.C., Library of Congress
  Joseph Alsop, papers
  John L. Balderston, papers
  Norman H. Davis, papers
  Cordell Hull, papers
  Breckinridge Long, diary
  William Allen White, papers
Washington, D.C., National Archives
  Department of State, decimal file (Record Group 59) (D/S)

III. MANUSCRIPTS: CANADA

Ottawa, Public Archives of Canada
  W. L. Mackenzie King, diary (microfiche)

IV. PRINTED PRIMARY SOURCES

Cadogan, Sir Alexander. *The Diaries of Sir Alexander Cadogan, O.M., 1938–1945*, ed. David Dilks. London, 1971.
Churchill, Winston S. *Complete Speeches, 1897–1963*, Vol. VI, 1935–42, ed. Robert Rhodes James. New York, 1974.
Forrestal, James. *The Forrestal Diaries*, ed. Walter Millis. New York, 1951.
Harvey, Oliver. *The Diplomatic Diaries of Oliver Harvey, 1937–1940*, ed. John Harvey. London, 1970.
Ickes, Harold L. *The Secret Diary of Harold L. Ickes*. New York, 1954, vols. II and III.
Jones, Thomas. *A Diary with Letters, 1931–1950*. London, 1954.
Lee, Raymond E. *The London Observer: The Journal of General Raymond E. Lee, 1940–1941*, ed. James Leutze. London, 1972.
Long, Breckinridge. *The War Diary of Breckinridge Long: Selections from the War Years, 1939–1944*. ed. Fred L. Israel. Lincoln, Nebr., 1966.
Lothian, Lord. *The American Speeches of Lord Lothian, July 1939 to December 1940*. London, 1941.
Moffat, Jay Pierrepont. *The Moffat Papers: Selections from the Diplomatic Journals of Jay Pierrepont Moffat, 1919–1943*. ed. Nancy Harvison Hooker. Cambridge, Mass., 1956.
Nicolson, Harold. *Diaries and Letters*, ed. Nigel Nicolson. 3 vols., London, 1966–68.
Roosevelt, Franklin D. *The Public Papers and Addresses of Franklin D. Roosevelt*. ed. Samuel I. Rosenman, vol. 9. New York, 1941.
USA. Department of State. *Foreign Relations of the United States*, 1940. 5 vols., Washington, 1955–61. (*FRUS*)

V. PRINTED SECONDARY SOURCES

Anderson, Irvine H., Jr. *The Standard-Vacuum Oil Company and United States East Asian Policy, 1933–1941*. Princeton, 1975.
Barron, Gloria J. *Leadership in Crisis: FDR and the Path to Intervention*. Port Washington, N.Y., 1973.
Beloff, Max. *Imperial Sunset: I, Britain's Liberal Empire*. London, 1969.
Blum, John M. *From the Morgenthau Diaries*. 3 vols., Boston, 1959–67.
Burns, James M. *Roosevelt: The Lion and the Fox*. New York, 1956.
——, *Roosevelt: The Soldier of Freedom*. New York, 1970.
Butler, J. R. M. *Grand Strategy, September 1939–June 1941*. London, 1957.
——, *Lord Lothian (Philip Kerr), 1882–1940*. London, 1960.
Casey, Lord Richard G. *Personal Experience, 1939–1946*. London, 1962.
Chadwin, Mark L. *The Warhawks: American Interventionists before Pearl Harbor*. New York, 1970.
Churchill, Winston S. *The Second World War*. 6 vols., London, 1948–1954.
Colville, Sir John. *Footprints in Time*. London, 1976.
Dallek, Robert. *Franklin D. Roosevelt and American Foreign Policy, 1932–1945*. New York, 1979.
Divine, Robert A. *Roosevelt and World War II*. Baltimore, 1970.
Farley, James A. *Jim Farley's Story: The Roosevelt Years*. New York, 1948.
Gilbert, Martin. *Winston S. Churchill*, vol. V, 1922–39. London, 1976.
Goodhart, Philip. *Fifty Ships that Saved the World: The Foundation of the Anglo-American Alliance*. London, 1965.

Hall, H. Duncan. *North American Supply.* London, 1955.

Henrikson, Alan K. "The Map as an 'Idea': The Role of Cartographic Imagery during the Second World War." *The American Cartographer* 2 (1975): 19–53.

Hull, Cordell. *The Memoirs of Cordell Hull.* 2 vols., New York, 1948.

Ions, Edmund. *James Bryce and American Democracy, 1870–1922.* London, 1968.

Johnson, Walter. *The Battle against Isolation.* Chicago, 1944.

Kendle, John E. *The Round Table Movement and Imperial Union.* Toronto, 1975.

Kimball, Warren F. *The Most Unsordid Act: Lend-Lease, 1939–1941.* Baltimore, 1969.

——. " 'Beggar My Neighbor': America and the British Interim Finance Crisis, 1940–1941." *Journal of Economic History* 29 (1969): 758–772.

——. and Bartlett, Bruce. "Roosevelt and Prewar Commitments to Churchill: The Tyler Kent Affair." *Diplomatic History* 5 (1981): 291–311.

Langer, William L., and Gleason, S. Everett. *The Challenge to Isolation, 1937–1940.* New York, 1952.

——. *The Undeclared War, 1940–1941.* New York, 1953.

Lash, Joseph P. *Roosevelt and Churchill, 1939–1941: The Partnership that Saved the West.* New York, 1976.

Leutze, James. "The Secret of the Churchill-Roosevelt Correspondence: September 1939–May 1940." *Journal of Contemporary History* 10 (1975): 465–491.

——. *Bargaining for Supremacy: Anglo-American Naval Relations, 1937–1941.* Chapel Hill, N.C., 1977.

Martin, Bernd. *Friedensiniativen und Machtpolitik im Zweiten Weltkrieg, 1939–1942.* Düsseldorf, 1974.

Matloff, Maurice, and Snell, Edwin M. *Strategic Planning for Coalition Warfare, 1941–1942.* Washington, 1953.

Medlicott, W. N. *Britain and Germany: The Search for an Agreement, 1930–1937.* London, 1969.

Nicholas, H. G. *The United States and Britain.* Chicago, 1975.

Osgood, Robert E. *Ideals and Self-Interest in America's Foreign Relations.* Chicago, 1953.

Pollock, Fred E. "Roosevelt, the Ogdensburg Agreement, and the British Fleet: All Done with Mirrors." *Diplomatic History* 5 (1981): 203–19.

Reynolds, David. "FDR on the British: A Postscript." *Proceedings of the Massachusetts Historical Society* 90 (1978): 106–110.

——. *The Creation of the Anglo-American Alliance, 1937–1941: A Study in Competitive Co-operation.* London, 1981; Chapel Hill, N.C., 1982.

Rhodes, Benjamin D. "Sir Ronald Lindsay and the British View from Washington, 1930–1939," in *Essays in Twentieth Century American Diplomatic History dedicated to Professor Daniel M. Smith,* eds. Clifford L. Egan and Alexander W. Knott. Washington, 1982.

Robinson, Edgar E. *They Voted for Roosevelt: The Presidential Vote, 1932–1944.* Stanford, 1947.

Sayers, R. S. *Financial Policy, 1939–1945.* London, 1956.

Sherwood, Robert E. *Roosevelt and Hopkins: An Intimate History.* New York, 1948.

Thompson, J. A. "From the Monroe Doctrine to the Marshall Plan." *The Historical Journal* 22 (1979): 731–745.

Thompson, Laurence. *1940: Year of Legend, Year of History.* London, 1966.

Tree, Ronald. *When the Moon Was High: Memoirs of Peace and War, 1897–1942.* London, 1975.

Watson, Mark S. *Chief of Staff: Prewar Plans and Preparations.* Washington, 1950.

Watt, Donald C. *Personalities and Policies.* London, 1965.

Wheeler-Bennett, Sir John. *King George VI: His Life and Reign.* London, 1958.

——. *Special Relationships: America in Peace and War.* London, 1975.

Woodward, Sir Llewellyn. *British Foreign Policy in the Second World War.* 5 vols., London, 1970–76.

VI. Interviews

Balfour, Sir John, London, 20 December 1975 and 14 January 1977.

Inchyra, 1st Baron (formerly F. R. Hoyer Millar), London, 8 November 1976.

Miller, Francis P. and Helen Hill, Washington, D.C., 27 April 1977.

Morgan, Aubrey N. and Constance Morrow, North Haven, Maine, 31 July 1977, and Oxford, England, 11 November 1979.

Rankine, Paul Scott, Washington, D.C., 4 May 1977.

INDEX

Admiralty, British, 26, 32, 44, 45
Astor, Lady, 4, 44

Balderston, John L., 33
Balkans, importance in Phoney War, 9, 13–14
Bases, US, on British territory, 26–30
Berle, Adolf A., 58
Blockade, British, of continental Europe, 10, 13, 38, 57
British fleet, possible loss of, 18–25, 28–30
Bryce, Lord, 1–2
"Burma Road," 35–36

Cadogan, Sir Alexander, 2, 5, 8, 10, 40, 45, 46
"Century Group," 31–33
Chamberlain, Neville (NC), 2, 8–10, 14–16
China, 35–37
Churchill, Winston S. (WSC):
    opinion of Lothian, 15–17, 39–40, 59–60
    correspondence with Roosevelt, 16–17, 27, 43–48, 54–56, 59
    and future of British fleet, 18–30
    and destroyers deal, 18–31
    policy towards USA, 25–29, 41, 45–46, 50, 58–59
    and British secrets, 25–26, 32, 45, 50, 59
    and Far East, 37
    and blockade, 37–38
    and origins of Lend-Lease, 39–56
    letter of 8 December 1940 to Roosevelt, 43–48, 54–56
"Cliveden Set," 4, 8
Colonial Office, 26–27
Craigie, Sir Robert, 35

Dalton, Hugh, 38, 39, 57
Davis, Norman H., 3, 5, 7, 17, 32
Destroyers Deal, 18–34
Dominions Office, 26

Election of 1940, USA, significance of, 40–43

Far East, 35–37
Foreign Office (FO):
    and Lothian's appointment, 2, 7–8, 58
    views on Lothian, 8, 10, 12–13, 15, 49, 51, 58
    and British commercial policy, 13–14

and Churchill-Roosevelt correspondence, 16–17, 44–47
policy towards USA, 10, 25–26, 40, 45
See also Destroyers Deal, Far East, Lend-Lease
Foster, John, 31
Frankfurter, Felix, 3

George VI, King, 5, 8

Halifax, Lord:
    selects Lothian as ambassador, 2–5, 7–8
    and USA, 10, 12–13, 14, 25, 40, 44, 46–47, 58
    and Churchill-Roosevelt correspondence, 16–17, 27, 46–47
    succeeds Lothian as ambassador, 57, 59
    See also Foreign Office
Harvey, Oliver, 2, 58
Hopkins, Harry, 17
Hull, Cordell, 20, 30–31, 37

Ickes, Harold L., 27–28, 53
Italy, importance of in Phoney War, 9, 13–14

Japan, 35–37

Kennedy, Joseph P., 10, 16–17, 25, 27
Knatchbull-Hugessen, Sir Hughe, 6
Knox, Frank, 27–28, 29, 36–37, 46

Lamont, Thomas W., 3, 55
Lampson, Sir Miles, 2
Layton, Sir Walter, 49
Lend-Lease, 40–56
Lindsay, Sir Ronald, 1–2, 3, 5, 6, 8, 10–11
Lippmann, Walter, 3, 5, 58
Lloyd George, David, 3, 8, 57
Lothian, Philip Kerr, 11th Marquis of (PL):
    appointed ambassador to USA, 1–2, 7–8
    achievements as ambassador, 1, 57–60
    qualifications for ambassadorship, 2–5
    relations with press, 3–4, 10–12, 31–33, 48–56
    religious beliefs, 3, 57
    policy towards USA, 4–5, 6, 9, 13–14, 25, 42–43, 45, 49–50, 58–59
    attitude to Germany, 4, 6, 8, 16, 22–23
    and "Cliveden Set," 4, 8
    and federalism, 4, 11–12

meeting with Roosevelt, 2 January 1939,
6–7
erratic judgment, 8, 21–23, 29–31, 35–
36, 50–51, 57
limited role during Phoney War, 9–14
speechmaking, 11–12, 15, 21–22, 33–34
and Churchill, 15–17, 39–40, 58–59
and Destroyers Deal, 18–34
Yale speech, 19 June 1940, 21–22, 28, 57
doubts about British chances in 1940,
22–23, 29, 35–36
leaks sensitive information, 31–33, 48–53
and Far East, 35–37
and British blockade, 38
and 1940 election, 39, 42–43
visits Britain in October-November 1940,
39–40, 43–45
and origins of Lend-Lease, 40–56
and Churchill-Roosevelt letter of 8
December 1940, 43–48, 54, 56
press conference of 23 November 1940,
43, 48–56, 57
death, 57, 59–60
Luce, Henry, 32

Mackenzie King, William Lyon, 6, 25
Mahan, Alfred T., 5
Merriman, Roger B., 7–8
Meyer, Eugene, 12
Ministry of Economic Warfare, 38
Ministry of Information, 52–53. *See also*
Propaganda
Morgenthau, Henry, Jr.:
and Destroyers Deal, 27–28
and Japan, 36–37
and Lend-Lease, 46, 49, 53, 55

Pan American Airways, 26
Perowne, J. Victor, 12, 15
Phillips, Sir Frederick, 40, 50, 52
Phoney War, 9–14

Propaganda, British, in USA, 2, 10–11, 32,
52–53
Purvis, Arthur, 44, 46, 53, 57

Reid, Ogden, 12
Roosevelt, Franklin D. (FDR):
and Lothian's appointment, 3, 5–8
meeting with Lothian, 2 January 1939,
6–7
correspondence with Churchill, 16–17,
27, 43–48, 54, 56, 59
and future of British fleet, 18–30
and Destroyers Deal, 18–31
doubts about British chances in 1940, 19,
23–25
and 1940 election, 24, 40–43
and Far East, 36–37
and British blockade, 38
and US entry into war, 41–43
and origins of Lend-Lease, 51, 53–56

Scott, David J. M. D., 12, 46–47
Shipping crisis, British, 40, 46–48, 53, 56
Staff talks, Anglo-American, 25–26
State Department, 5, 11, 13–14, 36–37, 58.
See also Hull, Welles
Stimson, Henry L., 27–28, 30, 36–37, 54
Sulzberger, Arthur H., 12

Thompson, Dorothy, 12
Treasury, British, 10, 44, 50. *See also*
Phillips
Treasury, US. *See* Morgenthau
Trevelyan, George M., 7–8
Tweedsmuir, Lord, 6, 7

Vansittart, Sir Robert, 2, 8

Welles, Sumner, 5, 30, 54
White, William Allen, 3, 31–33
Willkie, Wendell, 40, 42

PUBLICATIONS

OF

The American Philosophical Society

The publications of the American Philosophical Society consist of PROCEEDINGS, TRANSACTIONS, MEMOIRS, and YEAR BOOK.

THE PROCEEDINGS contains papers which have been read before the Society in addition to other papers which have been accepted for publication by the Committee on Publications. In accordance with the present policy one volume is issued each year, consisting of six bimonthly numbers, and the price is $20.00 net per volume.

THE TRANSACTIONS, the oldest scholarly journal in America, was started in 1769. In accordance with the present policy each annual volume is a collection of monographs, each issued as a part. The current annual subscription price is $50.00 net per volume. Individual copies of the TRANSACTIONS are offered for sale.

Each volume of the MEMOIRS is published as a book. The titles cover the various fields of learning; most of the recent volumes have been historical. The price of each volume is determined by its size and character, but subscribers are offered a 20 percent discount.

The YEAR BOOK is of considerable interest to scholars because of the reports on grants for research and to libraries for this reason and because of the section dealing with the acquisitions of the Library. In addition it contains the Charter and Laws, and lists of members, and reports of committees and meetings. The YEAR BOOK is published about April 1 for the preceding calendar year. The current price is $5.00.

An author desiring to submit a manuscript for publication should send it to the Editor, American Philosophical Society, 104 South Fifth Street, Philadelphia, Pa. 19106.